The **Professional Singer's Guide** to New York

by Richard Owens

American Institute of Musical Studies

Copyright © 1984
American Institute of Musical Studies
2701 Fondren Drive
Dallas, Texas 75206
(214) 691-6451

Library of Congress Catalog Card Number 84-70649

ISBN: 0-915357-05-4

Cover Design: Creative Images
in New York City
Produced by: Fred Weidner & Son Printers, Inc.

Research for this book was underwritten in part by a
grant from the Mobil Foundation

Contents

Part I.   Living in New York City

Part II.   Studying in New York City

Part III.   Auditioning

Part IV.   Working as a Singer

Appendix A—Education

♪ Welcome to New York! Whether you have just arrived at Port Authority, LaGuardia, Penn Station or elsewhere, you now are in the heart of the world toward which you have been working for years in college and graduate school. You are going to try to succeed in the profession that until now has been a distant dream, and you have come to the only place in America where you can really do it.

Where are you from? (People will ask that dozens of times.) Miami? Dallas? Topeka? Billings? Long Beach? No matter—you are now from New York. The shock of your new surroundings (did you see all those weird people at the terminal?) is severe. New York is exciting, but it is also scary. Forget "back home," because all your energy will need to be directed toward building your new life as a professional singer. This book will show you how to start working on your career in a step-by-step manner.

Some of you are old hands at managing life in New York City but are looking for new ideas. Many others have been here before and know your way around to some extent. Realizing that, we arranged this manual so that you can go straight to the information you need.

We at the American Institute of Musical Studies have been helping young singers for many years. It started when, as a sixteen-year-old baritone, I sang my first professional job. I was the young singer being helped, and the year was 1948. As an institution we have been in business since 1968, when we planned the first Summer Vocal Institute in Freiburg, Germany.

After fourteen years of helping American singers get started in Europe, it was time to give them a hand at home. We began in the fall of 1982 by presenting a seminar, "The Professional Singer's New York," at Hunter College. The seminar was a big success. Yet we needed something we couldn't find: a good handbook for the young professional—a directory of services, people and organizations, a guide providing sound advice for the first career-entry year. So we decided to write the book ourselves.

To achieve our goal, we began by calling upon AIMS alumni, many of whom are young singers who once needed the same kind of information, help and guidance as you. We asked them, "What do you wish you had known when you came to New York?" With this group of young professionals, we put together a task force to compile answers, solve problems and do a lot of homework.

Our book is not the first of its kind, however. Dr. Edward Dwyer's *Singers in New York* and Karen J. Smith's *The Informed Performer's Dictionary of Instruction for the Performing Arts* both preceded ours. We are indebted to both authors for their work, and we wish to acknowledge that some of our ideas can be traced directly to their pioneer efforts.

Personally, I wish to thank Lynne Dickey and Sandra Van Cleve, who did the legwork for this book. There would have been no book without them. Additionally, I want to express my thanks to all the "AIMSers" who helped, especially Connie Coit, Donna Wissinger, Elaine Linstedt and Don Price.

Professionally, we are honored that Barbara Sher was willing to contribute the chapter on networking for singers. We know that her assistance will be enormously helpful to young artists.

AIMS is deeply indebted to Mr. Donald J. Aibel, attorney at law, for allowing us to use the income tax record-keeping forms.

Finally, I must express my deep appreciation to my editor and friend Connie Stallings, who combined her personal interest in young artists with her professional expertise and helped to make a book out of my pile of notes!

Richard Owens

February 1984

Part I. Living in New York City

♪ If you have not yet decided to come to New York City, the following information may help you learn whether you are ready to make the move. If you
are already here, you may wish to skip this section and jump ahead to the
next one. But if you are now making plans to come, please read this section
carefully. It was written especially for you.

You should have both short-term and long-term goals as clearly in mind as
possible. Begin by determining where you are as a performer. Be objective.
For instance, if you are still having vocal-technical problems, your first goal
should be to find the right voice teacher and allow her/him to start you on a
program to correct the problems before you do any auditioning. Or, if you are
in great shape vocally but have had little experience performing, plan which
opera workshops to audition for. Additionally, you should have your long-range
goals in mind. Do you want to be acclaimed as one of the world's great voices
and call the Metropolitan Opera home base? Or would you rather be part of
a close-knit repertory company like the New York City Opera, which looks for
singer-actors? Or would you prefer breaking new ground with New York Lyric
Opera, which produces two or three modern operas each year?

Practically speaking, you will probably get a voice teacher *and* attend opera
workshops *and* do less prestigious types of singing. AGMA's executive secretary, Gene Boucher, emphasizes that singers shouldn't be too picky about
how they support themselves in their early years in New York. But it is well to
keep in mind where your heart truly lies, and to keep that end goal in sight.

Try to find a place to stay temporarily—preferably with a friend who cares
about you and your future. You will need at least a month to find your own
apartment or other place to live, so it is important to have a temporary base
of operations. It is also important to have someone giving you moral support
while you get adjusted to the city. If you can arrange to stay cheaply with a
friend and get some pointers and moral support at the same time, you will be
way ahead in the game. At the opposite extreme is the person who moves
into a hotel, spends more money than s/he can afford while apartment hunting
and is terribly lonely besides.

Have a job waiting. Obviously, this may not be possible. But many people
may be working for a company that has a New York office which can provide
them with a job in advance. If not, make use of any and all personal contacts
to arrange for a job ahead of time. Another alternative is to save as much
money as possible to give yourself a cushion while looking for employment.

Familiarize yourself with New York City before you arrive. Get a map and
study it. Learn where the five boroughs are in relation to each other, and
where Lincoln Center is located. Borrow copies of, or subscribe to, *New York
Magazine.* It is a wonderful source of inside information on the topics of most
interest to city dwellers.

Announce your impending arrival. Send postcards or letters to everyone
you know in New York, saying you are coming and that you would appreciate
their advice on places to live, eat, sing, and so forth. If you don't know anyone
here, draw on the friends and acquaintances of others. People will be your

greatest resource while making a career in New York (plus your own persistence and resilience, of course), and you should learn to accept their assistance. If is often true that achieving success in New York depends on "who you know." Making a career here or anywhere frequently is a matter of becoming known—in as positive a context as possible—to a large number of people in your profession. So give yourself a headstart and announce your arrival in advance.

Select a voice teacher and coach and make arrangements to study with them in advance. Consult your current voice teacher and coach for suggestions if you think that they are knowledgeable about study in New York. Or ask singers whose training you admire for the names of any good teachers they are aware of. If master classes at your local college or university are being taught by a prominent New Yorker, attend them to find out whether you would feel comfortable studying with the individual. If none of these alternatives is available, don't despair. Further suggestions about finding good vocal instruction appear later in this book.

Prepare yourself financially. You must realize that an artist is a small business. And any small business needs "front end" investment capital. To make the transition to New York, you will need a minimum of $8,000 to $10,000. Plan to earn and save that much by your mid-twenties. In the long run the savings might do you more professional good than attending graduate school. Make a budget for the first six months in New York. It might look like this:

Moving to New York
Transportation to New York (more or less) . . . . $ 400
Expenses in first week (allows for mistakes)   400

First six months
Apartment   2,750
Telephone, with machine or service   700
Food, including dining out twice weekly   2,080
Clothing (you'll need to buy some)   250
Transportation   300
Lessons   2,600

                                                               Total $9,480

After living in New York for three months, you should be re-earning most of the money. Then you can bank at least $4,000 for future expenses or emergencies.

We realize that it won't be possible for everyone to accomplish all of the above. But at the very least everybody can think through the first item and should make a stab at the last one. They will make the transition much easier.

♪ Congratulations are in order—to you. You have accomplished something that many singers never have and never will. You have had the courage to move to New York to try to make a career as a professional singer.

Did you know that most people with degrees in voice never get this far? They convince themselves that they could not reach or survive in New York; then they never escape the marriage/children/jobs/teaching syndrome. You are special because you have cut loose and started where the majority would not. You have demonstrated courage and ambition. Never forget it! There will be times ahead when you will doubt the wisdom of your move. When the going gets tough, don't ask yourself, "Why did I ever come to New York?" Say instead, "This is harder than hell, and I am miserable, but I am proud that I am trying to do what I want. I have not given up my goal." That will remind you of your worth, even though your desired career may not seem to be getting off the ground.

Now, as you are beginning your career, we want to recommend a book that will be a tremendous resource: Barbara Sher's *Wishcraft*. It provides an excellent plan for organizing the way to build your career and will help you make decisions. Additionally, it will keep you going when you are ready to quit. Buy the book and read it and, especially important, do the exercises in it.

We believe that one of the biggest problems for a singer in New York is psychological—how to stick with a goal and stay sane when the goal seems unattainable. One way is to feel good about who you are and what you are doing. Mentally healthy people are able to handle adversity far better than sick ones.

Think about your supposedly unattainable goal. What is so difficult to get? Fame? A contract at the Met? Money? All may be difficut to attain, but lack of these elements does not cause failure in the singing business in New York. Rather, these elements are the results of being a successful singer or are the signs of success. It is how to reach these goals, or how to approach them, that is so bewildering.

We believe that every problem has many parts. Once you break down your problem into separate parts, you suddenly see things you can achieve prior to attacking the core of the problem. It is our premise that a career in singing can be planned and pursued in an intelligent, reasonable manner. And the first step in the process of career-planning is to select out those components over which you have control and go to work on them.

♪ Kurt Vonnegut calls New York "the capital of the world." When one speaks of the arts, especially music, that is one hundred percent correct. No city is more important for music and musicians than New York. Regional opera in the United States has grown, but New York is still king and will be for years. For the sake of your career, you have chosen the right place. But New York is also expensive, dirty, frustrating, competitive, bewildering and even dangerous. It is "no place to bring up a family," according to many. Still, it is the center of American musical activity, and you must eventually live here to become a successful performing artist in the American music business.

Books and Maps

When you move to New York City, learn as much about it as you can. Study its history, life-style, great cultural and recreational assets and physical layout. The layout may be the most important, at least in the beginning, because if you cannot find your way around the city, you will waste a lot of time and money, and you will miss out on a great deal. We strongly suggest you purchase a map and a guidebook. That may sound a bit "touristy" to you, but they are absolute necessities. Look up the five boroughs, the important areas of town, the major buildings and how to get around.

The Hagstrom Map of New York City is probably the best and most detailed map. It includes all streets and even some building numbers, so you can zero in on the exact block of any numbered address. Bus and subway routes are shown, but without identifying route numbers or letters. This map is available at all major bookstores.

A different kind of map, and the one the cab drivers use, is a small inexpensive publication called *Flashmaps: Instant Guide to New York.* It contains fifty maps that are cross-indexed with 3,000 listings; also subways, buses, museums and restaurants. Once you get the hang of how to use the cross-indexing, it's terrific. A young singer we know from California claims that *Flashmaps* is the only thing she's ever found that keeps her from getting lost south of 14th Street. Available from bookstores and newsstands.

Many guidebooks are available. A recent count at a midtown bookstore totaled forty-six! Two we recommend are the *Michelin Green Guide to New York City* and the *American Express Pocket Guide to New York* by Herbert B. Livesey. They contain useful information about museums, theaters, hotels and restaurants, as well as maps. Both are available at most bookstores.

Another type of book that will be invaluable is a money-saving guide. We recommend *Bargain Finder: The Encyclopedic Money Saving Guide to New York City* by Eric Zuesse. It lists the best bargains in all the boroughs. Additionally, it contains sections on services of all varieties, on neighborhoods, on apartment finding, on what to do when things go wrong, and on good restaurants, entertainment and maps. All entries are rated for being low in cost but high in quality. At a list price of $4.95, the book is worth its weight in high C's.

Other Sources of Information

Free information on the city is available from the New York Convention and Visitors Bureau at Two Columbus Circle, New York, New York 10019. You can walk in and pick up travel guides and maps of the five boroughs, information on theatrical and cultural events, hotels and restaurants, and other subjects. The largest source of free information is the New York Public Library, the main branch of which is located on Fifth Avenue at 42nd Street. As a singer, you should be aware of the Library and Museum of the Performing Arts at Lincoln Center, whose street address is 111 Amsterdam Avenue at 65th Street. The entrance is to the right and slightly behind the front of the Metropolitan Opera House. Anyone living, working or studying in New York is entitled to a free library card.

Transportation

The next step is to learn the transportation systems, of which Manhattan has four: subways, buses, taxicabs and feet. (You will walk more in New York than in any other city in the United States.) You can pick up a map of the subway system and of the bus routes at any subway token booth or at the New York Convention and Visitors Bureau.

Subways. Subways are the fastest form of transportation if they go where you want to go and if that is more than fifteen blocks. They are also dirty and crowded and often dangerous. (See "Personal Safety," below.)

Buses. Buses are less stuffy and safer than subways. You can usually see where you are going and get off if it turns out to be wrong. Buses are much better than subways for crosstown (east–west) travel. When boarding, you can ask for a transfer to another bus at no extra charge.

Taxicabs. New Yorkers use more taxicabs than any other folks in America, and maybe the world. But unless you have the money, use taxis sparingly. They cost one dollar to begin with, plus ten cents per one-ninth mile traveled and/or forty-five seconds of waiting time. In heavy traffic a cab can be slow and expensive.

Feet. Your feet can take you many places for less money than any of the above. Walking is great exercise and helps to keep you trim. If you have the time and the weather permits, you should walk. But you will need better walking shoes than you have ever owned.

Personal Safety

Never forget that New York, along with all its wonderful attributes, is full of crime. Your next task, before you start moving about the city, is to become streetwise. That word describes the person who knows where s/he can safely go and how to take care of oneself when there. The best and most complete discussion of this subject probably is contained in the paperback entitled

Street-Smart: The Guardian Angels' Guide to Safe Living by Curtis Sliwa and Murray Schwartz. The language is heavy-handed, but the ideas are right on target. From it you can learn to be aware of what is going on around you, wherever you are, and to provide yourself with margins of safety and cushions of space.

♪ Finding an apartment in Manhattan—and by this we mean more than just a roof overhead, basic plumbing and a bunch of quarrelsome roommates— is highly challenging. How much should you pay? Where should you live? It all seems to be a huge problem. We advise you to look for a place which you can afford and which will support your development as an artist (that is, which does not include many anxiety-producing distractions).

What you pay and what you get in return in New York City bears no resemblance to any other place in the United States or other civilized (or uncivilized) countries. Particularly in Manhattan, you will pay a great deal more for much less space and fewer amenities than elsewhere. Five hundred dollars per month might provide the penthouse suite in San Angelo, Texas, or Carthage, Illinois, but in Manhattan it will rent (if you are lucky) a tiny one-room fifth-floor walk-up in a dingy building in a seedy part of town. But don't get discouraged yet.

Keep in mind what compensates for the high rent: easy access to the most exciting, culturally stimulating city in the world. For a singer New York City is the hub of the universe for employment opportunities. Though the competition is proportionately fierce, all the auditions here take place within a small radius. If you hustle, you can probably do two or more a day. That would be impossible elsewhere.

Give serious consideration to living in adjacent New Jersey, Brooklyn, Queens or the Bronx. Rents there are often one-half to two-thirds of Manhattan rents. Many of the neighborhoods are safer, more attractive and closer (by subway or PATH train from New Jersey) to midtown Manhattan than are many areas in Manhattan. You really, truly will not fall off the edge of the earth by living one subway stop into Queens. Living in another borough or in New Jersey presents no serious disadvantages to a singer. It need be as little as ten minutes away from any audition or performance. The only difficulty is in people's minds. Manhattanites have a tendency to feel self-sufficient and smugly isolated from all life beyond the Hudson and East rivers; they imply that beyond those magic borders lies a gaping void. They are wrong, of course, and struggling singers will do their pocketbooks a great service by not succumbing to that view.

The easiest and perhaps the worst way of finding an apartment is to use the services of one of the apartment referral agencies listed in *The New York Times.* Do not do this unless you have exhausted all the other ways of locating an apartment.

Here are some suggestions for finding a place to live in New York City, in order of decreasing desirability. As you will see, the idea is to use as few intermediaries are possible.

1. Ask anyone and everyone you know or meet in the city about any apartments opening up that might meet your needs. Ask these people to ask their friends, as well.

2. Select some neighborhoods that appeal to you and walk around them for an hour or so, looking for *For Rent* signs and asking people in the

neighborhood to identify the owner of any likely-looking building. Then contact the landlord directly and ask if any apartments are coming vacant in that building.

3. Check bulletin boards at the following places:

a. The schools (New York University, Columbia University, Manhattan School of Music, The Juilliard School, Mannes College of Music, and so forth);

b. The unions (AGMA, Equity, SAG, AFTRA) if you are a member. All these places have bulletin boards where you can look for listings or post one of your own;

c. The Metropolitan Opera and New York City Opera. Both have bulletin boards accessible to the general public.

4. Check the newspapers. New York newspapers list available housing under many categories. These include: *For Rent*—furnished and unfurnished, *Sublets* or rentals for a limited time (be careful; the current occupant may be subletting unlawfully, without the landlord's permission), *Shares, Co-ops* and *Living Lofts.* Additionally, you might check the *Help Wanted* ads under the *Household Help Wanted* section for positions offering some combination of room and board (even a salary, sometimes) in exchange for companionship, babysitting and/or light housekeeping.

The Village Voice is probably the most promising newspaper. It comes out once a week, on Wednesdays, and runs many of the city's most reasonable offerings, many of them non-agency. One of the reasons is that running an ad in the *Voice* costs approximately one-tenth as much as running a similar ad in *The New York Times.* Other good bets are neighborhood papers like the *Chelsea-Clinton News, Queens, Greenpoint Gazette* and *The Phoenix* (Brooklyn), which charge even less for advertising and usually limit their ads to a certain area. So if you know an area where you'd like to live, learn the name of the local newspaper and check its real estate section. Additional possibilities are the trade papers: *Backstage* (probably the most popular and the best), *Variety, Show Business* and *Billboard.*

Then there are New York's daily newspapers—*The New York Post, The Daily News* and *The New York Times.* People find good apartments through these papers, but it is wise to be very selective because of the large number of agencies advertising in them. Hint: The Sunday Real Estate section of *The New York Times* can be purchased at some newspaper stands as early as Friday and if you go directly to the *Times* office, perhaps even as early as Thursday night. Since any really good offerings are snapped up almost immediately, it is worth buying this section ahead of time at the paper's full price to get the jump on all the other apartment hunters.

5. Check into various types of temporary housing. The YWCA and YMCA are good bets, as are some comfortable and moderately priced hotels. There is an excellent section on these hotels in the book *Bargain Finder.*

6. Try one of the Roommate Referral Services listed in the Yellow Pages or newspapers. The fee is usually paid by the person looking for a place to live, not the person who has the apartment and wants a roommate. All the

services claim to screen applicants for compatibility, but it is said that they frequently don't try very hard. So don't expect to find a perfect roommate at the first few places you are sent. Hang in there until you find a suitable situation.

7. <u>At the bottom of the suggestions barrel, use an agency</u>. Call or write The City of New York Department of Housing Preservation and Development, Office of Development, 100 Gold Street, New York, New York 10038, telephone (212) 566-6510. Ask that you be sent the list of public-subsidized housing, with the names, addresses and phone numbers of the agents who manage each development. The waiting lists can be long—for some, a couple of years—but applying may be worthwhile because public housing affords some of the most reasonable, high-quality housing in the entire city. Other housing agencies are far less reliable. Beware of exorbitant fees, advertised apartments that don't exist, finder's fees and paying anybody anything without getting a legitimate lease or legal document in exchange.

Safe Neighborhoods

There are certain neighborhoods in New York that you may want to stay out of entirely for safety's sake. But even in these neighborhoods many blocks are being rehabilitated, so "good" and "bad" blocks can be found back to back. For years people have considered Harlem unsafe. Yet middle-class respectability has been steadily working its way up the East and West sides. Now many of the old prejudices about Harlem carry little weight. The same can be said about the Lower East Side and some parts of the notorious South Bronx.

For more complete information about safe neighborhoods you might read "The City's Safest Neighborhoods" in the October 19, 1981, issue of *New York Magazine. Bargain Finder* contains excellent material on the subject. Author Eric Zuesse makes the suggestion that before committing yourself to living in an area, you should phone the local police precinct and speak with the crime-statistics officer about the relative safety of the block you have in mind. And once again you should use all your personal contacts. Try to get specific information, not just rumors.

As a footnote to this discussion, we mention that the upper middle West Side (the area west of Central Park from the 50s through the 80s and even the 90s) is the center of the music world, revolving around Lincoln Center at 63rd Street and Broadway. Most voice teachers and coaches, and many singers, have studios and apartments in this area. Unfortunately, rents have risen very high, and the greater affluence of the residents has attracted increased crime. Still, it is a lively and attractive neighborhood, and singers can't be blamed for electing to live there despite rising costs.

Health Care

Another important aspect of living in New York City—especially for singers—is adequate health care. Because of the nature of your profession, there will be times when you need to get well more quickly than other people, and stay well. Undoubtedly many competent ear, nose and throat doctors practice here (see the listing of otolaryngologists in the Yellow Pages), but three well-known ones seem to care for many singers:

Wilbur James Gould, M.D.
47 E. 77th Street
(212) 879-6630

Eugen Grabscheid, M.D.
49 E. 96th Street
(212) 289-4550

Leo P. Reckford, M.D.
640 West End Avenue
(212) 877-2386

♪ Singers have the grandest dreams of all. They want the brass ring, and they're willing to work for it. For years they structure and discipline themselves like athletes in training for the Olympics, and one day they are ready. Many of them decide it's time to take on New York. Then, as they are left on their own, the structure of the years of preparation disappears. Unaffiliated singers looking for success move in a world which has no support system of any kind and is highly competitive, full of rejection and frequently beset with financial hardship. How can they keep believing in themselves and in the brass ring? How can they stay in good voice, in good spirits, optimistic?

Last spring, as this book was being written, a group of singers got together to discuss such questions.

Sandy said, "The problem is keeping up your morale, remembering that you are an artist when the world seems to have forgotten, being willing to go out and audition in a good frame of mind, being good-natured about supporting yourself doing work you didn't choose after having spent years training for work you're not doing." Everyone nodded agreement.

"The best thing to do," said Barbara, "is complain loudly and then get on with it. Let's draw up a list of why it all seems hopeless on our blackest days." Everyone contributed some terrible things they believe when morale is sagging.

1. I'll never get enough money or leisure to keep studying.
2. Self-doubt climbs in the window when I'm sleeping.
3. I have no self-discipline. Can't stick to a daily regimen. Have trouble concentrating.
4. I feel sorry for myself too much.
5. I'm too self-critical.
6. I think too much and act too little.
7. There isn't enough emotional support in my life.
8. I didn't receive the best training when I was young.
9. I must not be ambitious enough; otherwise I'd always feel positive.
10. I hate auditions!
11. I'm too old. (This came from the youngest person in the room.)
12. I'm not a good enough musician; I always make some error in learning music.
13. I'm not a good-enough actor.
14. I'm too lazy.
15. I can't stand the tension.
16. I'm too fat, too thin, not pretty enough.
17. I'll never be good at languages.
18. My diction will be imperfect forever. (Applause from the group, and rueful laughs.)
19. I want a nice home and children.
20. I don't have the time and patience to keep corresponding with opera companies as I should.
21. I have personal or technical problems no one else has.

By then each singer was laughing and blushing a little, glad to know that everyone felt the same way occasionally. Then it was on to the solutions. One by one they described how they coped.

Elaine came to New York two years ago, stayed with a friend until she got a typing job, then moved to her own apartment. Not being a good typist, she didn't enjoy her job much, but it paid the rent. She began to develop a sideline as a seamstress, and that turned out to have some real benefits: after a while she left her typing job and was able to arrange her own time. An unexpected plus was that she found herself in an excellent bartering position and learned how to swap her sewing skills for some of the best coaching available. "I visited good coaches and carefully looked for frayed collars and missing buttons," she grinned. Now she practices daily and keeps in good physical shape.

"But it wasn't easy to get into this pattern," Elaine commented. "I had to deal with many morale problems. That list we just made could be all mine. Before I came to New York, I had been working steadily. I was a success and accustomed to it. The difference here was very hard to deal with."

Because Elaine doesn't work in an office, she has an additional problem: procrastination. She must structure her time or get lost in procrastination, which can cause "the worst feelings imaginable." She made a five-year plan. In five years, she expects big results. Her way of achieving her goal is to build her network base. She is doing that in many ways, but the major way is being heard as often as possible by as many of the right people as possible.

"I've set myself the challenge of auditioning as often as I can. Rather than worrying about not getting chosen as I used to, having an excellent audition is my goal." It's paid off. She has begun to receive calls because of recommendations made by people who heard her a year or more ago.

Elaine's five-year plan is her biggest morale booster. But she has a way of taking care of each day, too. She does aerobic dancing to a record every morning. It makes her feel wonderful and always restores her perspective. Every day she sets aside some time to treat herself. She'll take a walk, read a favorite poem or meditate. Then she does whatever she needs to do for her singing.

"And in the evening," asked Lois, "when the light is failing and everyone else is sitting down to dinner with their big families and hospitalization plans?"

"I call a friend," Elaine replied.

Which brought the group to the next major requirement of surviving: affiliation. Young singers in New York are, often for the first time, unaffiliated. The difficulty that creates is hard to explain. Most come, stay with a friend at first, and then find their own apartments and their own jobs. Then they go looking for coaches. Then auditions.

Sandy said, "Nobody talks to us, and we don't talk to anybody. At the end of a long day you can wonder if you really exist. Sometimes the only way you know is because you feel so bad."

"I advise absolutely every New York-bound singer to remember how to stay in touch with people," Karen exclaimed. She picks up a phone and calls an acquaintance when she's feeling isolated, a practice that has turned many acquaintances into real friends. She phones even when she's feeling fine— for ideas, advice, problem solving or going to a movie. Where does a singer meet these people?

"Take extension classes at Mannes or Manhattan School of Music, or Juilliard or at any university in town," said Karen. "It doesn't have to be in music; it can be in languages, history or anything. And talk to the people in the classes. It will make all the difference in the world."

Sandy suggested churches, saying, "New York churches have really tried to meet the needs of people who come here from other places. I've found some wonderful people." Other members of the group agreed, and the following lists were quickly made:

Places to look for extension classes
> The New School
> New York University
> Columbia University
> The Network for Learning
> The Learning Annex

(Note: Addresses and additional schools appear in Appendix A.)

Places to look for group activities
> Unitarian Church of All Souls
> Park Avenue United Methodist Church
> St. Bartholomew's (Episcopal) Church
> The local Y

At this point, Vivian commented, "I haven't felt more constructive and less alone in ages than I do right now. And I have a family here in New York. An ongoing version of what we've been doing this afternoon—admitting our feelings and giving each other moral support—could make everything so much easier."

So here's our major recommendation to young professionals: form a support team of some kind and make sure it gets together every week or two to air problems and share solutions. Complain if you need to, and release the negativity. Laugh at it. Think of ideas to help each other or anybody else in your position, because each of you is valuable to all of you. Singers are the most intelligent artists around. You can teach each other how to maintain the courage needed to aim for the top.

And if reading these pages has helped you arrive at additional personal solutions, send them to us. We'll share them with other singers in future editions of this book.

♪ Ouch! The Big Apple takes a big bite. New York City is expensive—"mega-bucks," as the teenagers say. Rent and transportation alone take a huge chunk of money; eating in a restaurant can wipe you out in one evening. What can be done?

To begin with, you should not come to New York broke. (We know, this is great advice if you are still in Topeka, but useless if you are sitting in your apartment on the West Side.) As we said before, if you plan to move to New York, you should save between $8,000 and $10,000 to get you started. Here are a few ways to raise money, and a few ways to save it.

You should purchase a few paperbacks on financial subjects. You need one good underground-type shopping guide (see Appendix B), and you will need some tips on taxes. And you should make a personal budget (see Chapter One).

You must learn very early to be an enthusiastic fund-raiser for yourself. You will have to convince people to invest in you and your career. To do that you must be convinced you are worth the investment, and be willing to share your commitment with potential supporters. Your confidence is part of your belief in yourself as an artist and should manifest itself in everything you do—not just in performing.

We have seen singers raise thousands of dollars to enable them to attend AIMS' Summer Vocal Institute in Graz, Austria. Some receive help from foundations, some from a single donor, some from relatives, some in the form of loans, and some in a number of gifts—as small as fifty cents. There are as many ways to raise money as there are singers. But you probably have not been taught how to do it, nor has anyone explained that it is a basic part of being an artist. You need to form an image of yourself as a complex piece of artistic technology which, though dedicated to performing, has a built-in arts administration staff: artistic director, business manager, development officer/fund-raiser, secretary and press agent. If you want to continue to be a performer, you must make all these roles function in your behalf.

Raising money in the form of grants, gifts and scholarships is not terribly difficult, but it requires much planning and real work. In New York City you should begin at the Foundation Library (see Appendix B), where you can become acquainted with the fund-raising routines that are currently practiced. After doing your research, begin applying for some specific grants that suit your profile. The experience will be well worth every hour invested.

As your next step you should visit the New York Public Library, where you can read about competitions (enter them for the money, not the experience), grants (especially the impressive National Opera Institute grants) and apprentice programs. Most of the important competitions and grants are listed in "Career Guide for the Young American Singer" published by the Central Opera Service. Then start contacting the appropriate organizations. But the process takes time. You cannot do it all in your first month in New York City.

A word of caution: If you have saved the $8,000 to $10,000 mentioned above to start your career in New York, do not spend it all in your first year!

Put away at least half of it. It is better to work now as a waiter or waitress and have a reserve money fund available later when you'll need it more. Examples: You may discover you need money to go to Europe to start your career. You may need time and money to prepare for a recital debut that comes from winning a major competition. You may get a really good engagement in the Midwest and need money to prepare for and travel to it. We hope you get the point.

♪ Singers tend to be a bit short-sighted when it comes to working outside their own profession. They are unaware of how gifted they are! There are a host of jobs available to well-groomed, attractive, personable young people, especially if they are skilled. We strongly recommend that you learn a few skills that are much in demand today.

The list of important artists who came to New York with a second profession is endless. Diction coach and tenor Nico Castel sold toilets for American Standard. Producer Hal Prince assisted a professional artist. Conductor and coach Joan Dornemann taught music. Sherrill Milnes taught school. Can you type? Can you operate a word processor or a computer? Do you have an engineering degree? Or one in accounting? Good, because you will most definitely need those skills.

There are several advantages to beginning a career in New York with a second profession. It gives you the chance to become acquainted with the music world before taking that final leap. You can make many business and social contacts, which will advance your singing career more rapidly. And then there's that important income.

If you have typing skills, try working as a "temporary." But don't register with just one agency and wait for it to call you. Every business in New York is competitive; you must be, too. Register with four or five agencies and call them repeatedly until they give you some work.

On the subject of job hunting, we strongly recommend that you read *What Color Is Your Parachute?* by Richard N. Bolles. This book will not only help you find a job, but will help you understand yourself and your potential in your profession.

Financial Management

It is important to start learning to handle your finances and taxes well if you have not done so already. In New York you will be earning far too little money to pay Uncle Sam more than absolutely necessary. Our first recommendation is to get a good tax advisor. (See the list of tax consultants who are familiar with artists' problems, in Appendix D.) S/he will save you money and time.

Our second recommendation is to learn to keep records. In Stephanie Winston's book, *Getting Organized,* there is a basic plan for organizing financial records. As an artist you can deduct an incredible amount from your taxes, but that will not do you any good if you have no papers as proof. Part IV. of this book includes a fuller discussion of taxes and a long list of deductible items.

Part II.   Studying in New York City

♪ One reason many singers come to New York City is to study. Being a world center of professional music, New York has a concentration of talented and experienced artists and teachers who can teach tremendous amounts to young singers.

The AIMS seminar, "The Professional Singer's New York," is designed not only to help singers learn to get into the music business, but to help people in the business get into teaching.* At a recent seminar, Metropolitan Opera tenor and diction coach Nico Castel said, "You must keep in sight the fact that even though you are singing and earning something you should not stop growing." Studying will be a major part of your life in New York for a long time. So learn to study well at the beginning.

You should consider several aspects of your study program. First and foremost, naturally, is your choice of voice teachers. Almost equally important is your choice of vocal coaches. But there are other areas of study that are absolutely necessary to artistic growth. Diction, acting and languages are all vital to your development. And no matter how many of those courses you had in college, their quality was not professional enough for the big time. Additionally, you may need such specialty studies as fencing, dancing and mime, along with personal growth classes and courses about the business end of our profession.

Several critical areas of study are discussed in the next three chapters.

---

*The AIMS seminar, "The Professional Singer's New York," is offered annually in the early fall. For details, write or call: AIMS, 2701 Fondren Drive, Dallas, Texas 75206; (214) 691-6451.

♪ In New York an estimated 800 persons are currently teaching voice! As a young artist, you are confronted with this overwhelming number of choices when you begin your search for that important person who will help you perfect your technique, inspire you to perform better and provide entrée to famous conductors and impresarios who might give you a job.

Traditionally, a new voice teacher is found in several ways. S/he might be:
• Recommended by the singer's teacher back home (often the teacher's teacher),
• The teacher of one's best friend in the city,
• Recommended by a well-known personality, perhaps someone who taught a master class,
• A teacher made famous because of her/his students, or
• A teacher known for her/his books and articles.

The problem with the above methods is that they may not take your individual needs into consideration. For instance, the teacher of your teacher back home may teach the same method, but if you failed to master the method in the previous four or five years of training, it may not be the way for you to learn. Or, perhaps you have had enough of it and need something totally new to develop your voice in a different direction. In any case, we suggest that you consider a different approach.

The first step in finding a teacher should be "know thyself." Take the time to analyze your own voice. Establish where you are in your vocal growth and where you need to go next. Listen to ten or more good singers in your Fach to discover what you cannot do yet. *You should be looking for a teacher who can take you beyond where you are now, not keep you comfortable with it!*

Once you have established what you need to accomplish, you can begin your investigation. Ask your friends, other singers, your coach, anyone, to answer some specific questions about teachers. Examples: I want to work on the break in my middle register—does Teacher X do that? What teacher do you know who works with evening out the scale of the voice? Who are some of the singers Teacher X has worked with?

You will get many answers, some only partially true. But try to keep in mind precisely what you are looking for. Some friends may comment that you don't need what you think you do (a nice compliment); others may say that it can't be taught (which is nonsense—anything can be taught); still others will have no comments or answers.

Keep asking until you have the names of at least six possible teachers. Get as much information on each of them as you can. (Consult this book's Appendix A.) Listen to their singers who are currently performing. Meet some of their students and talk with them. Attend a lesson, if the teacher allows it, and observe what is going on. Be willing to pay a fee to observe because you will, after all, be getting instruction.

Once you have gone through the above steps for at least four teachers, you can start narrowing down the field. You will have to weigh the pluses and minuses. Expense is important, but don't cheat yourself out of a career just because of the price of voice lessons. Convenience, compatibility and other points also must be considered as you make your decision.

Then go to the teacher and make a candid contract. "I want to study with you for X months to improve my vocal technique and to work expressly on the breaks in the middle register in my voice." If the teacher is honest, s/he will agree to your contract or to a reasonable variation.

At the end of X months—we advise that you spend at least four with any teacher—check on your progress. Compare earlier recordings with the way you sound now. Ask your friends and coaches if they can hear a difference. If the responses are negative, ask the teacher about your progress. If s/he cannot give you a straight answer, it is time to move on. Hire another teacher to work for you.

The above approach may seem a bit cold to singers accustomed to working in a business where mere personal contacts have value. Nevertheless, considering the number of artists who fail to establish careers, we feel it is time to urge newcomers to abandon some of the old methods and learn to act on their own in a more independent manner.

Our List of Voice Teachers

The list of voice teachers in Appendix A includes teachers from colleges and universities, members of the National Association of Teachers of Singing and New York State Teachers Association, private teachers and performing singers who teach also. We have tried to list as many teachers as possible. We know the list may include some charlatans and frauds, but it includes many honest pedagogues who may be helpful to you. Read the codes carefully and ask for references. If a teacher is paranoid about supplying them, s/he may be a poor choice as a teacher.

For your enlightenment, we have marked with three asterisks (***) the teachers whom we at AIMS have worked with and know to be effective. Lack of asterisks means simply that we know about the individuals only through our questionnaire. But we have omitted any teacher whom we know cannot be recommended. Of course, the omission of several hundred others who are unknown to us should not be taken as an indication of disapproval.

♪ A vocal coach works with a singer on her/his understanding of the music, both structurally and stylistically, and of the text or dramatic situation. A coach helps you make music out of a group of notes, helps you make sense when you sing, helps you find repertoire suitable to your talent. A coach provides you with an experienced musical foundation upon which you can build and project your musical and dramatic personality. On a more basic level, a coach teaches you how to perform your repertoire properly, with good diction, appropriate tempi, suitable dynamics and correct style. Most coaches are pianists or conductors.

Not all coaches are good for all things. Many singers will work with one coach on French repertoire, another on Italian opera and still another on oratorio. It would be impossible for any coach to command all areas of the repertoire equally well. Therefore, singers can spend a great deal of money while preparing their entire repertoire. For that reason, we recommend that you find a good pianist/accompanist who can help you, less expensively, learn your notes and work on your coach's suggestions.

Our List of Vocal Coaches

The list of accompanist/coaches in Appendix A was compiled from questionnaires sent to coaches whom we already knew and from recommendations by various singers and teachers in New York. It includes both experienced coaches who have worked in major opera houses and young pianists who are just beginning accompanying careers. Unfortunately, there is no organization of coaches which will provide us with a suitable list of names in the profession, so our list is not as long as we would like.

We have marked with three asterisks (***) the coaches whom we at AIMS have worked with and know to be effective. Please read the codes carefully before attempting to use the list. AIMS cannot accept responsibility for everyone whose name appears.

♪ Today there are many pressures on the young artist to be a "singing actor" or "acting singer." But both these terms are inadequate to describe what producers and stage directors are really looking for. They seem to want someone who can act with the stage knowledge of Judith Anderson, sing well in all styles of opera, operetta and musicals, and be alternately as laid back as Dean Martin or as intense as Maria Callas. We believe it is impossible to be or do all these things, but we do know that every young singer needs to spend more time developing dramatic capabilities. To that end, we have sought out New York classes in acting and listed them for you in Appendix A.

Members of our task force attended some of the classes listed so we could more accurately report on what transpires in a session. Unfortunately, many other listed classes could not be experienced personally by a member of the group. Again, please read the codes carefully.

Part III.   Auditioning

♪ Auditioning in New York City poses the same problems and instills the same fears as auditioning elsewhere, except they are worse. If you failed in Peoria, only a limited number of relatively unimportant people (sorry, Peoria), professionally speaking, know about it. If you fail in New York, though, that's it—or at least, so it seems. In any case, whatever one's problems are with auditioning, they will be magnified in New York.

Let's examine the auditioning process and see if we can learn how to audition better and how to plan for successful auditions.

Perhaps we can tame the audition monster by cutting it up into manageable pieces. As we said in Chapter Two, we operate on the premise that almost every aspect of a singing career can be planned and prepared for so that one's chances of success are as great as possible in relation to one's talents.

The Fear Factor

At a recent AIMS seminar, Joan Dornemann, the Metropolitan Opera coach, prompter and conductor, spoke on auditioning. As her first point, she chose to discuss the question, "How do I get rid of my nerves?" Her response was, "If any of you has an answer to that question, I want you to tell me right now!"

We all have problems with nerves and fear. It is part of being an artist and exposing one's creative self in public. Or, as Barbara Sher puts it, "Fear is the natural companion of creative action." How well we *perform* with our nerves and our fear, though, is what matters. As far as the public is concerned, the performance is more important than what goes on behind it. This truth is especially valid for auditioning because the auditioners are looking for results. Let's examine how fear applies to auditioning.

The auditioning process instills fear in five ways:
1. fear of being ill-prepared,
2. fear of not being good enough,
3. fear of the unknown in the auditioning situation,
4. fear of the people hearing the audition, and
5. fear of failure to achieve the goal toward which the audition is directed.

Let's face it: fear is real. Denying that will only cause it to manifest itself in an unpredictable manner, so accept the reality. But at the same time, you should realize that some fears are imposed by you yourself, while others are caused by the situation. If the factor that causes a particular fear is controllable, advance planning can allay that fear.

Fear No. 1: Of Being Ill-prepared

The fear created by being ill-prepared is the easiest fear to deal with because it is possible to prepare almost everything about an audition. Obviously, music can be prepared well, but lack of other preparations can cause fear and nervousness. How many singers go to an audition with a new piece that they have never performed? How many go without having a rehearsal? How many go without deciding what to wear or without planning transportation?

An example of good preparation appears below. The steps may seem obvious to you, but those who are eternally disorganized should find them helpful. Let's assume that you will be auditioning for the annual Metropolitan Opera Regional Audition, since that is an experience almost every singer has at one time or another. The auditions are usually held in late winter and spring, so you begin preparations after Labor Day.

Sept. 10 Discuss your repertoire with your teacher and begin working on twice the number of arias needed. Provide for any vocal growth that may be occurring, but retain your old repertoire along with the new in case the vocal improvement or change is not complete by the time of the auditions.

Sept. 15 Do your homework on all your arias. Study the plots of the operas, translate every word precisely, memorize all the texts, take them to your diction coach and to your vocal coach. Get as many good professional opinions as possible so you can feel confident that you have made the best decisions, adjusting any ideas as necessity dictates. After committing texts and music to memory, take the arias to your acting class and begin working through the dramatic situations.

Oct. 1 Get a brochure and application blank (write the Met for the nearest audition place, the rules and so forth) and read it carefully. Begin gathering any necessary papers (birth certificate, letters of recommendation, etc.). Make a duplicate of the application blank and fill it in; later, fill in the blank itself and mail it.

Nov. 10 Set a date to preview your audition materials. Invite eight or ten friends to hear you do your thing. (Invite only friends. You won't need any "objective" opinions for this purpose; only sympathetic listeners.) Serving a little wine and cheese might make the occasion festive. Ask whether your coach's or teacher's studio can be used (it's probably bigger than yours) or rent a hall (see Appendix C for the amazingly low prices of some New York halls). Before singing each aria, tell your friends why you chose it and how you feel about it. Afterward, listen carefully to the feedback about what sounded best and made the best overall effect. You might record both performance and feedback for future study.

Dec. 5 Time to sit down with your teacher and coach and eliminate any repertoire that is unnecessary, add any variations and make any final cuts. Between now and Christmas, work intensely to bring all your repertoire up to its optimal level.

Dec. 15 Be careful! The period around Christmas and New Year's is dangerous for a singer. There are usually extra concerts and engagements to sing,
and your life rhythm can change drastically, especially if you go home for
the holidays. Immediately after the holidays a physical letdown often occurs,
so allow for it and be especially nice to yourself during the first week of
January.

Jan. 2 As soon as possible, carefully get your voice in shape so that by
January 15 or 20 you are better than you were in December. The critical
time when you will begin competing is approaching.

Jan. 5 If you are a member of an audition group, try out all your materials as
often as allowed. Get your audition so routine that nothing can go wrong.

Jan. 15 Write down, step by step, what you will do from two days before the
competition until you *win at the finals.* Begin by making sure you have all
the correct information about the people, dates and places. Then walk
through everything you'll do on the day of the competition. Go by the hall
where it will be held. Check out the transportation system you'll use. Figure
the time you'll need to get to the hall, allowing for bad weather and any
other hindrances.

Jan. 25 This is a good time to cry. Get mad, fight a little with your teacher
and coach, and bring out any lingering doubts or problems. Then during
the last ten days, concentrate on building your self-confidence. Bathe yourself in compliments; spend time only with supportive people.

Feb. 13 Two days before the audition, get everything ready. Get your clothes
ready. Get your music ready; even get your apartment ready. On day before,
rest. Sing only as much as you need to and don't test your voice. (It has
been ready for weeks!) Reward yourself for being well prepared by treating
yourself to a new score, a chocolate sundae, a long-distance call to a good
friend or some other nice thing.

Feb. 15 On the day of the audition, get ready normally but allow a little extra
time for everything. Before you set out, do an imagery exercise. Picture
yourself going into the hall and meeting the people in charge of the competition. See them liking you. See yourself running into your friends who
are entering, also your rivals and enemies. Get rid of any ill feelings about
them now so you will not be thrown when you see them backstage. Picture
your accompanist being glad to see you and ready for your rubati, ritardandi,
fermate and cuts. Now picture yourself on stage announcing your numbers.
Your voice is stronger than you had expected. You are insanely nervous,
but it is not affecting your voice. Hear yourself singing well—no matter what
the order of your audition . . . Now congratulate yourself on having done a

wonderful job. See yourself practically floating offstage! And above all, *see yourself winning!* You deserve to, for you did your absolute best. Everything about the competition that you could control has been a success. You are a winner already!

Fear No. 2: Of Not Being Good Enough

The fear of not being good enough requires a different treatment from that above. Preparation is measurable, tangible; being "good enough" is questioning one's very being, or so it seems. To ask, "Will I be good enough?" is to question all of life. But try inspecting this phrase to find out what prompts your fear. Ask yourself, "Good enough for what?" "Good enough for whom?" And, "What is enough?"

Jennie Tourel, the great mezzo-soprano, was a very dear friend. But I once made the crude mistake of asking this great lady of diminutive stature, "Jennie, how tall are you, anyway?" since the subject had often been discussed. The dramatic fire in her eyes burned through me as she pulled herself up to her full height and bristled back, "Tall enough!" I never asked her again. The point I wish to make with this story is that the word "enough" often seems to be interpreted as "barely adequate." But let's clean up our English and realize that it means "fully, absolutely and irrevocably the exact right amount." Pavarotti and Domingo are good enough to be the two best tenors in the world. Rather than having barely achieved professional status, they are good enough, and that's terrific!

Let's examine also the "for what" and "for whom." Begin with where you are today and decide what is possible realistically before tonight. In other words, forget the fantasy world of being in the middle of an advanced career as a major operatic artist in London, Vienna, New York and Paris. You are a young, comparatively unknown singer living in a small New York apartment. Are you up to today's tasks? Can you practice today in order to sing for your coach the phrases that were studied at your lesson yesterday? To put it simply, you should not expect yourself to live up to impossible standards.

As we said before, your fear will be greatly lessened if you will approach the individual, conquerable parts of the process separately and not the whole problem at one time. If you are good enough at each individual step in the learning process, you will be good enough at the end.

Fear No. 3: Of the Unknown

Is the next fear—fear of that which you do not know or understand—really any different? It should be conquerable by following the step-by-step procedures outlined above. Ask yourelf, "What is it that I do not know?" Make a list—literally—of everything you do not know about a given audition. After a little research, you will be able to answer 95 percent of the items listed.

Perhaps you are planning to sing in the Metropolitan Opera Regional Audition. One of your fears may be, "I don't know what I will sound like in the hall." Now think a minute. Is it possible to practice in the hall? Is it possible that the hall in question is similar to another where you can practice? Can you talk with singers who have sung in the hall? Can you attend a concert or rehearsal there and go backstage to familiarize yourself with it? And so forth. The point is that this kind of fear can be allayed with good information, and you can do enough research to get the information.

But what about fear of that which you *cannot* know? "Will they like me? Will I be in good voice? Who else will be singing?" Well, if you want to make up a long scare list of possible threats, go ahead. Please understand, though, that spending time on fearing that over which you have no control is not only wasted energy but mostly in your head. It is like worrying about the weather or the Mid-East crisis. You can't control it; you can only hope for the best. *So don't frighten yourself by letting unknown or unpredictable factors control your feelings, your courage or your confidence.*

Fear No. 4: Of People Hearing the Audition

The fear of people hearing the audition is one of the craziest. For some reason, singers often tell themselves, "He is so important that he scares me!" For the word important, you could substitute, quiet, cold, loud, blustery, or whatever. Most of this kind of fear is also in your head.

Now, don't misunderstand. If you are singing for James Levine for a Metropolitan Opera contract, he is *very* important. You should have great respect for him and his authority (not to mention his artistry), but he has two arms and legs like any other human being. Your fear is not of him personally but, once again, of unknown factors. Therefore, follow the same procedure as above. Separate your fears into those items that can be researched and conquered, and those over which you have no control.

Fear No. 5: Of Failure—or Success?

Fear of failure is the worst fear for a singer. But is it really failure you're afraid of? You know a lot about failure. If you are an American, you have been conditioned all your life to be a good loser. You have friends who will welcome you back after the audition and go to dinner or a bar and feel badly with you. You also probably have a family which will be understanding.

We suspect that your real fear is of being a success! What will happen if you are a winner? Will you be lonely? Won't your friends feel jealous or left out? What will happen if you have to sing on the stage of the Metropolitan Opera House? Will you know how to act? Are you good enough? (That last question sounds familiar.) Won't your life change drastically?

What you do now is sit down and work out a game-plan for "Phase Two." You have a new set of goals to attain. And you go about reaching them in the same manner you employed before. That is how to banish fear of success.

We hope that this chapter will help you organize a clear pattern of planning for, working toward and attaining your auditioning goals. Auditioning is like any other task; when it is broken down into its solvable parts, the unsolvable ones become unimportant. There is a procedure to follow. There is specific homework to do. There are short-term goals to reach. There are daily battles to win. There is the promise, and the risk, of becoming a winner!

♪ All singers should follow a few personal rules about auditioning which have to do with professionalism. You should make up your own personal set of rules and hang them on the wall, but herewith are some ideas.

Accessibility. You must be available when people want you. If you do not have an answering machine or answering service, you can forget auditioning. In Appendix D we have listed some telephone answering services which we have found to be satisfactory.

Dress. Learn how to dress for auditions. It will be different from the way you dress for doing radio jingles! Develop a few contacts with people whose taste in clothing you admire and get some feedback on your wearing apparel.

Know your auditioners. Some of the silliest mistakes can be made when you are not aware of the importance (or unimportance) of the person you are singing for. Always research the identification and background of the person who will hear you.

Keep records. Keep records of what you sang for whom and when, what you wore, where you sang and who accompanied you. Additionally, keep a record of the results. That should help you to see any patterns. Appendix F includes a sample audition record-keeping form.

Resumes. Don't waste money on expensive resumes, but make sure yours are presentable. The more concise, the better. Include only important information and be neat. For most auditions, one or two pages is plenty. Appendix D includes the names and addresses of two resume services which can help make your resume appropriate.

Pictures. You must have decent photographs. But again, don't waste money on anything fancy. (Later, when you are making more money, you can indulge yourself.) Be sure your name is on your photos. (Our files are full of lovely singers' faces with no names!) Appendix D includes a list of several dozen portrait photographers.

Practice auditioning. Above all, get accustomed to practicing auditions. If you practice them regularly for almost anyone, you will always be ready, even on short notice, and you will have less reason to be nervous.

Part IV. Working as a Singer

♪ New York City abounds with opportunities to perform, but like everything else here, those opportunities must be sought out. Our first advice to someone seeking performance opportunities would be to say, "Don't pass up anything, because you never know *who* might see you perform." In a recent seminar on professional singing in New York someone mentioned that after every performance you should write thank-you notes to the conductors with whom you sang to help them keep a good feeling about working with you and your vocal capabilities.

Do you have a mental block against singing showcases? Do you despise Broadway show tunes? Do you hate jingles? Can't sight-read? Get rid of all that. In New York there is a saying, "If it pays well, do it!" There is much work in synagogues and churches, and many opera singers have supported themselves singing in Broadway choruses while pursuing operatic careers. As long as you are not hurting yourself technically, there is nothing wrong with pursuing other types of singing. You are a performer. And *performers perform,* not just take lessons. You must be out there, feeling the response of an audience, getting reactions to your performing and your materials.

The Recital

Once you get started in New York, one of the easiest ways to perform is to do a recital. In the city there are numerous recital halls and other appropriate places, such as churches, mansions and museums. Most of the museums screen their applicants carefully; for them you must submit a resume and sometimes an audition tape. If you do not get an invitation from a church or museum, we suggest that you produce your own recital. There is no better way to start a support group, to experience the reactions of an audience or to learn about the business. But first do your homework.

Do you have a program that fits your performing needs, or do you simply have a program of songs that you like to sing? What you like and what sounds best are sometimes different. Have you tried out your materials on friends or family? Before deciding to sing an aria on a recital, you should sing it for someone. *The Art of the Song Recital* by Shirlee Emmons and Stanley Sonntag is excellent. Read this book thoroughly and make careful, calculated decisions about your own recital. It need not be big, expensive or extravagant, or reviewed. But you are in the business to perform, so do something nice for yourself—perform!

Church Positions

Singing in church comes naturally for most singers, because a majority began that way. If you are from rural or small-town America or anywhere in the South, Midwest or Northeast, you probably did much of your early singing in church. In New York church singing can help to make your living, and it is important to learn soon how to do it well. Getting a church job is not in itself difficult. Getting one in Manhattan, as opposed to Westchester County or another outlying area, is a little more difficult. Getting a high-paying church job is more difficult still, especially when you are a newcomer. As you learn the ins and outs of the church singing business, though, you will improve your position and marketability. Here are a few points to consider.

Auditioning. To audition for a church job you must perform some good standard oratorio repertoire. Of course you must know *The Messiah* and *Elijah,* but you should know three or four other standard works, too, and you should familiarize yourself with major oratorios that might not have been performed in your local church. For instance, the Bach *Passions* and the Mozart *C-Minor Mass,* which are really standard, are not necessarily done in small churches. You would do well to learn at least one major selection from one of the *Passions.* Sopranos should know the "Et incarnatus est" from the *C-Minor Mass* and the "Exsultate, jubilate" (but most people are tired of hearing the "Alleluia" alone as an audition piece).

The other major need in auditioning for church jobs is being a good sight-reader. Many churches in New York hold their rehearsals immediately prior to the service, and they must have singers who can perform the music immediately. If you are not a good sight-reader, it is very important to begin practicing it right away. At auditions for church jobs you will almost invariably be asked to sight-read.

Agents. A few agents specialize in placing singers in church jobs (see Appendix E). This practice may seem strange to people from the Midwest or South, but it is an absolute necessity in a city with hundreds of church positions and several thousand professional singers. There is no more convenient way to make a church connection than through an agent. Agents hear auditions regularly, so you need only call. Your audition must include standard oratorio excerpts and sight-reading; be prepared. Note that some of the church agents handle bookings for oratorio and choral jobs, also, so ask about that when you register with them.

Locating a Position. The simplest way to find a suitable church job is to go through an agent, as described above. Nevertheless, you may want to find a job on your own. In that case, see Appendix E, where we have listed most of Manhattan's religious institutions that engage professional singers. Select one near you and try it, or pick one of a particular denomination. You might attend a service to make sure you like the pastor, priest or rabbi, and the music. Afterward, speak with the music director and arrange an audition. It might even be wise to sing on a volunteer basis for a while to get your foot in the door.

Your Faith. Normally the nature of your faith will not make any difference in being hired. Yet you will be asked occasionally, so be prepared for this eventuality. Additionally, you should be aware that you may be confronted with ideologies you don't agree with. Do you want to participate in religious activities that run strongly counter to your own beliefs? It may not make any difference one week, but it can make an entire year of singing every Wednesday, Friday, Saturday or Sunday very uncomfortable. Only you can make the decision. Think this through carefully before accepting the position. As a professional, it behooves you to behave in a professional manner, regardless of the institution's faith or denomination. If you cannot adjust to participating in it, you probably should not be there.

Languages. Singing well in English is an absolute necessity for church and oratorio singing. The words must be understood. If you have any problems with your diction, you should begin work on them right away. It is also mandatory that you sing in proper ecclesiastical Latin and in both modern and traditional Hebrew. If you don't know Hebrew, learn it, for it will increase your ability to do synagogue and temple jobs easily.

Money. Many church jobs pay barely more than transportation. If you have a job in Westchester County which pays $35 a Sunday and has a rehearsal during the middle of the week, you may not make enough money for the job to be worth your while. You might be better off singing at a church in Brooklyn that pays $25 but rehearses just before the service. Additionally, take into account your own personal needs for study time before committing yourself to an extended contract with a church.

Quality. Even though we in America are proud of the country's generally high quality of amateur music-making, you may work in churches with people who are not as well trained as you are. After all, you are a member of an elite group: you have at least two degrees, have devoted years of practice to your profession and know your craft quite well. Now you may confront a musician who has been on the job as an amateur and whose training was only rudimentary. Once again, as a professional you must learn to adjust to this situation or, if you cannot adjust, learn to avoid it.

Vocal Problems. Perhaps the church choir director will require a method of singing that is incompatible with your technique. Some choral conductors simply do not understand the human voice, or they demand harmful execution. It is imperative that you learn immediately whether singing in any church or other choral organization is going to hurt your voice. If the director demands a straight tone, for instance, and that is hard for you to achieve, singing there is probably not worthwhile because it would run counter to your vocal work during the rest of the week and would retard your growth as an artist. Or if the conductor requires very loud singing and you are a light soprano or tenor, that too could be detrimental to your vocal health. Choral singing is not in itself hard on the voice, but bad vocalism is, and you must decide whether you can sing well within the existing framework of the church.

Choral and Oratorio Organizations

For many years singers have traditionally earned money in New York by performing with professional choirs. There are not as many choral groups now as there were twenty or thirty years ago, but several professional choral jobs are still available. Regardless of whether a job pays, there is a great deal to be learned about the choral business in this city. The major New York choral organizations are listed in Appendix E, but think about these basics before getting involved with any of them:

Meeting People. Any young singer in New York finds it difficult to meet people. Both the Oratorio Society of New York and the New York Choral Society are organizations with large memberships which afford the opportunity to meet many other singers. Additionally, they enable you to expand your knowledge of music styles and of various conductors.

Professional Contacts. Choral jobs afford professional contacts at a very important level. For instance, you can request an audition for a solo position with anyone who has conducted your choir. Observe his conducting manner at a rehearsal. If you decide you would like to sing for him, speak to him during a break or after rehearsal. Say you want to audition and ask when he could hear you. Then follow through with a letter and a resume so that he will have written information about you. This is one way of becoming acquainted with potential employers and may be your best avenue for getting established in New York.

Touring. Many choral organizations tour with their performances, although not as many as did a few years ago. Some tours are extensive, going cross-country or abroad; others go simply to outlying areas in the metropolitan region. One important fact to remember is the difficulty of maintaining a regular church job while touring. After being selected for a professional tour, it is always disappointing to learn that your church job will not release you. You might plan for this ahead of time by selecting a church where there is some freedom to have substitutes or be absent occasionally.

Listings. Before Easter and again at Christmas *The New York Times* publishes a listing of almost all the oratorios being performed in the city, including conductor, location and price. You should study these listings carefully, attend some performances and write letters to the appropriate conductors. This can be a slow process, but it should be part of your ongoing attempt to become better known.

Opera-Performing Organizations

In addition to the Metropolitan Opera and the New York City Opera, New York has a multitude of smaller opera companies. They are listed in Appendix E, along with a brief description of their kind of repertoire and the names of the people in charge. We strongly suggest that you begin attending performances of these organizations because performances will tell you more about them than anything else. Some may seem outrageously amateurish. Yet many of the most famous singers at the big opera houses began by performing with these very companies. Besides, just because a company has some amateurish aspects does not mean that you have to be likewise. You need experience, and these companies may be where you can get it.

You might have heard that the way to get an audition is to contact a company by phone and then follow through with a letter and resume. In fact, it will probably be harder than that. You will have to be on the lookout for public announcements for auditions because most companies do not have budgets or staffs large enough to inform you personally when one is scheduled. Telephoning the company once a year is not enough. You must plan on staying in touch on a regular basis.

Remember that no matter how good a singer you are, New York is full of other good singers. You may audition again and again for jobs with these companies and be turned down, not because you are inferior but because there are many people who also are good. In some cases your voice may be better, but another singer has worked with the company before so the company feels secure in casting her/him. This is frustrating, but someday *you* will be the one they know and feel secure in casting. So don't allow yourself to become discouraged because you are turned down the first two or three times. (If you do, you are apt to quit before you reach your goal of becoming a full-time professional singer.) It may take several years of perseverance and many repeated hearings before your unique ability will stand out and put you ahead of the competition. Establish now a way of measuring the success of each audition and of identifying the competition so that you can know exactly where you stand in relation to the other singers. Be sure to make use of the audition record-keeping form in Appendix F.

It may be that you have not yet learned how to demonstrate your talent in an audition. If you are having trouble, we suggest that you return to Chapter Twelve, read it again thoroughly and apply the system to each of your opera company auditions. We are certain you will get good results eventually!

AIMS regularly holds seminars in auditioning techniques, and several audition classes are available in New York City.

♪ Obtaining management will be an important step in your professional career. That is a matter in which you have little expertise because most colleges teach nothing about it. Therefore you may want to enroll in an appropriate course in New York City. The Mannes College of Music and Manhattan School of Music both have courses related to the business of music that include information on management.

It is important to understand what a manager does. A manager "goes between" you and potential jobs. Her/his function is to advise you, arrange auditions and help find you jobs. Nevertheless, the truth of the matter is that you yourself will find most jobs in the early stages of your career. And you must understand that until you have a significant number of engagements, no manager may be interested in you.

When are you ready for management? Matthew Epstein, a vice-president of Columbia Artists Management and formerly one of the country's leading managers, says simply, "When you have something to manage." He means when you have enough engagements so there are problems working out your schedule and travel plans, when you have to make decisions regarding which engagements are better for your career, when you have to consider repertoire's appropriateness for you. If you have only one engagement a year for one role, then you hardly need anyone to manage it for you, and you certainly cannot afford to pay anyone 10 percent of the fee.

Another answer to the readiness question is given by Elizabeth Crittenden, also of Columbia Artists: "When you are marketable." You are ready for a manager when you are a saleable item—when people are interested in hearing you, when you have good reviews and recommendations, and when you have some good performing credits. At this point a manager may participate in your career because he can make money selling you.

Finding a manager can be a time-consuming process. If you are completely new to the business, we suggest that you begin by looking at the annual issue of *Musical America* (see Appendix B), which you can obtain at major libraries. It contains lists of all the managing organizations in the United States, along with their rosters, and reports from each organization describing its activities. Read these reports to get a feeling for what each office does.

Looking through *Musical America,* you may find a friend who is being managed. Then ask your friend about the manager and their relationship, whether it is a good office, whether the manager actually gets employment for your friend, and whether the management will hear new singers. Or as you read the annual you might figure out which managers are working with people like you. A management that has a list of mostly young artists will probably be more approachable than a gold-plated agency with only famous stars on its roster. Or you might read the annual to find out which agency manages the fewest singers in your vocal category, since that might influence its choice of you as a client.

Most New York managers hear a great deal of music in the city. If you are performing somewhere and want a manager to come, write to him and invite him. You may have to do this many times, but it is one of the ways of letting him know that you are active and are interested in working with him.

Most managers hear auditions regularly, so you should try to set up an audition with the manager of your choice. The process is simple: Send a letter with a picture and a resume and follow through by telephoning. You may have to call many times; persevere, but without being pushy. If you are unsuccessful, contact another manager. You may have to try several before one accepts you for an audition. But no manager can sell you if you are not yet ready, so you must complete your studies before you start looking for a manager.

You should be very wary about a few aspects of management. For instance, some managers charge a retainer fee—a front-end payment from you to work on your behalf. We think that it is seldom a good idea to work with a manager who charges a retainer fee. If, however, you choose to do so, make sure that your contract spells out clearly what the retainer fee covers and what you will receive in return.

If you have had no luck after several months of trying to find a manager, it is probably a good idea to try to get engagements, instead. Time spent arranging for auditions with conductors, directors and producers will bring you far more income and result in more activity than continuing to seek out a manager. When you get a large number of engagements and begin performing a great deal, a manager will probably seek *you* out, anyway.

We have not listed managers in this book because their names are readily accessible in the annual issue of *Musical America.*

♪ It is vital for professional singers to understand how the tax system relates to their profession. In the first years of your career you will earn too little money to allow for losing any unnecessarily by omitting deductions from your taxes. Also, you will be in no position to pay heavily for mistakes in the event that your taxes are reported incorrectly. As a beginning singer, *the most important thing you can do is to learn to work with a good tax consultant.* Tax consultants rarely cost as much as they save. In Appendix D we have listed several, all of whom we believe to be knowledgeable in the field of taxes for artists.

We call your attention to a series of articles by Harry Linton and Marc Bernstein in *Backstage* in January and February, 1983. Entitled "Actors and Income Tax," the series covers many areas of taxation for artists. We hope that *Backstage* will publish similar articles on a regular basis. Meanwhile, you can refer to the back issues in libraries and get information from a good tax consultant. (Linton and Bernstein, incidentally, are included in Appendix D.)

Deductions

The number and variety of deductions for the professional artist are amazing. For example, all of the following are deductible:

Answering services
Stationery and postage
Rehearsal studio rental
Makeup
Wigs
Hair dye
Hair care for the profession
Complete costs of photos, resumes and publicity
Union dues
Wardrobe maintenance (with exceptions)
Trade papers
Professional publications
Local transportation
Gifts to certain people
Professional research
Scores
Musical arrangements
Backstage tips
Promotional theater tickets
Beautification expenses
Drama and coaching lessons
Voice lessons
Fees to agents and managers
Dance clothes (such as leotards)

Cleaning of professional apparel (such as dance clothes)
Tapes, records, tape recorders (must be depreciated)
Professional advice and career guidance

A cursory glance down the list should reveal that there may be more to the business of taxes than you know about.

The deductibility of education depends on the timing. While you are in school, professional or otherwise, the cost of your education is not deductible. Your parents cannot deduct the cost of your college training, nor can you. When you become a working professional, however, many if not all your educational activities are deductible. Voice lessons, dancing lessons, acting lessons are quite normal deductions for professionals. Even dieting may be deductible if your manager or some role requires it. Here again, a good tax consultant is the person to show you how to take advantage of these deductions.

Keeping records

There are thousands of small items for which you theoretically should have receipts, but which are difficult to keep track of, such as taxicab rides, music paper, small supplies, and so forth. Primarily, you should keep receipts or canceled checks for all items that cost $25 or more. Checks are preferable and easier to keep track of. The exception to this, according to Linton and Bernstein, is that you must have a receipted bill for a time when you are working away from home and staying at a hotel, since the bill is only way to prove that the room was in your name and that you did not pay someone else's bill with your check.

When touring, you will need to make a record of all expenses, and all of them are deductible. You should save the receipts for major expenditures costing $25 or more, even though you may not have receipts for the small items.

Telephone calls can be averaged. If you audition a great deal and have to check in with your answering service or agent several times a day, you might spend up to $2 a week for telephone calls made while away from your apartment. Over a 52-week period that would amount to $104. You might be able to deduct this amount if you put it on the proper schedule in your income tax. On the other hand, you might not be able to make the deduction if you word it improperly. Your tax consultant can help you.

Of course, there are standard things about income tax which apply to all of us. You should have your W-2 forms. Sometimes they are difficult to obtain because you perform with several different organizations during the year. Even if you do not receive all the W-2s, make sure you keep track of all your bank deposits so that you have a record of your earnings. Your tax consultant can tell you what to do about lost W-2 forms and employers who are no longer in business.

Income averaging

Income averaging is one aspect of taxation that can be very favorable to the artist. To do it, though, you must have your tax returns from previous years in proper order. If you are newly in the singing business, income averaging may not be possible, but it is certainly worth a try. Incidentally, if you are new you had best make sure you can call yourself a professional singer before you report your taxes on that basis. This is particularly true if you have worked primarily as a secretary, teacher or something else and have just entered the profession.

We know from personal experience and from the experience of many artists that taxes are a problem most of us do not like to mess with. We can only say that there are people who will "mess with your taxes" for you and probably save you money at the same time. Use them!

Each of the individuals in the following list was sent a questionnaire requesting the information in the code. As much of the supplied information as possible appears in each entry. We have marked with three asterisks (***) the people whom we at AIMS have worked with and know to be effective.

Code

NAME   Professional name

ADDR   Current address and telephone number

PFFL   Professional affiliations, including unions, learned societies and/or positions with professional companies

TLOC   Coaching location if different from address above

AFFL   Academic affiliations, including colleges and institutes where currently teaching

LANG   Languages taught or coached

DAYS   Days when coaches

LENG   Length of lesson

COST   Cost of lesson

INIT   Is there a fee for initial interview or audition? (Y = yes, N = no)

ACMP   Is accompanist provided, and if so, is there an additional fee?

NEWS   Are new students being accepted?

PERF   Are performing opportunities provided?

FAME   Famous or well-known students

EDEX   Educational background and performing experience of coach

COMM   Comments

NAME   ALEXAY, ALEXANDER
ADDR   404 E. 55th Street, New York, NY 10022   212/355-4776
PFFL NYSTA, AFM Local 802, vice president of Bellemsans; **AFFL** Sakuyo Un Musashino (Japan) in July, Aug. & Sept.; **DAYS** Mon.–Sat., evenings &

weekends, Oct.–June; **LENG** 45 min; **COST** $25; **INIT** N; **ACMP** Self; **NEWS** Y; **PERF** Professional engagements, auditions, etc.; **FAME** Piano—Marie De Bernardo—Town Hall, Carnegie Hall recitals; **EDEX** Yoko Okai (Tokyo) recitals. Studied piano with Emil v. Sauer & Von Andbasfy at Vienna Academy. Accompanist—Richard Tucker, Jarmila Novotna, Conrad Thibault, Jan Peerce, Jerome Hines.

COMM Visiting professor of Voice—Sakung University—Musashino Music College, Kunatachi University in Japan (July, Aug., Sept.).

NAME   ALTMAN, MILLARD
ADDR   2061 Broadway, New York, NY 10023   212/874-1633
PFFL Metropolitan Opera; **AFFL** Manhattan School; **LANG** E, F, G, I; **DAYS** Mon.–Fri., days only; **LENG** 1 hr; **COST** $40; **INIT** N; **ACMP** Self; **NEWS** Y; **PERF** None; **EDEX** Juilliard School—Piano; Jonel Perlea—Conducting; teacher Manhattan School & L.A. Conservatory; assistant conductor, Empire State Festival, Pittsburgh Opera, Philadelphia Grand Opera, Hartford Grand Opera, Wagner Touring Opera.

NAME   BECKWITH, DANIEL M.
ADDR   115 W. 104th Street, #32, New York, NY 10025   212/864-1794
PFFL Coach, Carnegie Hall Opera series; AFTRA, AGMA, AFM Local 802; **LANG** E, F, G, I; **DAYS** Evenings & Saturdays; **LENG** 1 hr; **COST** $20; **EDEX** B.M., M.M., Westminster Choir College. Santa Fe Opera, Spoleto Festival USA, Spoleto Festival Italy, Michigan Opera Theater, Dayton Opera. Recipient of NOI grant as coach & concert accompanist.

NAME   BEEGLE, RAYMOND***
ADDR   12 W. 72nd Street, New York, NY 10023   212/724-5615
COMM Specialist in Russian diction & music.

NAME   BLIER, STEVEN
ADDR   344 W. 84th Street, New York, NY 10024   212/873-9111
PFFL Chautauqua Institution, Summer Music School head coach; **LANG** E, F, G, I; **DAYS** 7 days, evenings & weekends; **LENG** 1 hr; **COST** $25; **INIT** Y; **ACMP** Self; **NEWS** Y; **PERF** None; **FAME** Linda Zoghby, John Cheek, Paul Sperry, Catherine Malfitano, David Holloway; **EDEX** B.A., Yale University. Studies at Juilliard School with Martin Isepp. Currently regular accompanist in vocal studio of Marlena Malas. Aspen Music Festival ('78–'81). Private coaching with Janine Reiss.

COMM Specialties: French art song & opera, recital repertoire preparation & performance.

NAME BOOTH, THOMAS***
ADDR 400 W. 43rd Street, Apt. 30-S, New York, NY 10036 212/279-3054
PFFL COS, Phi Mu Alpha, American Symphony League, AFM Local 802; **LANG** E, F, G, I, S; **DAYS** Mon.–Sat.; **LENG** 1 hr; **COST** $30; **INIT** $30; **ACMP** Self; **NEWS** Y; **PERF** No; **FAME** William Walker, John Alexander, Carol Bayard, Richard Fredricks, Geraldine Decker, Batyah Godfrey, Justino Diaz; **EDEX** B.M., Trinity; M.M., TCU; conductor, Western Opera Theater, Orchestra da Camera of L.I., Opera Classics of N.J., Michigan Opera Theater, Opera Omaha, Baltimore Symphony, San Francisco Symphony, San Antonio Symphony.
COMM Caramoor Festival, St. Luke's Chamber Ensemble; also sing professionally; these additional abilities give my coaching added dimension.

NAME BRIDSTON, DANIEL***
ADDR 76 St. Marks Place, #3-A, New York, NY 10003 212/505-0595
AFFL Staff pianist at AIMS Summer Vocal Institute in Graz, Austria; **LANG** E, F, G, I, S; **DAYS** Sun. & Thurs., evenings & weekends; **LENG** 1 hr; **COST** $20; **INIT** Y; **ACMP** Self; **NEWS** Y; **FAME** Carol Vaness, Warren Nimnicht
COMM Lieder, aria coaching, German, French, Italian diction.

NAME BUTCHER, NAN
ADDR 360 E. 50th Street, New York, NY 10022 212/759-2243
PFFL NYSTA; **AFFL** Turtle Bay Music School—accompanist; **DAYS** Mon.–Fri., some evenings; **LENG** 1 hr; **COST** $20; **INIT** $10; **ACMP** Self; **NEWS** Y; **PERF** None; **EDEX** B.A., Grinnell College, special courses at Chicago Musical College, N.Y.U., Juilliard. Accompanied singers at many N.Y.C. recital halls.
COMM Besides a classical background, I accompany for a musical theatre workshop & have been musical director for many cabaret shows & musicals. The workshop is at Turtle Bay; I highly recommend it.

NAME CASTEL, NICO***
ADDR 170 West End Avenue, New York, NY 10023 212/799-8014
PFFL AGMA, AFTRA, NATS, Metropolitan Opera; **TLOC** Above and at Metropolitan Opera; **AFFL** Mannes, N.Y.U., Long Is. Univ., YMHA School of Music, SVI, Santa Fe; **LANG** E, F, G, I, P, S; **DAYS** 7 days, evenings &

weekends; **LENG** 1 hr; **COST** $35; **INIT** N; **ACMP** If desired; **NEWS** Y; **FAME** Shicoff, J. Morris, Malfitano, Elvira, Monk, von Stade, Blegen, Battle, Ewing.
COMM Tenor & artist member of Metropolitan Opera. Also official diction coach for Metropolitan & associate professor at N.Y.U.

NAME CHURCH, JOSEPH
ADDR 144 Willow Street, Brooklyn, NY 11201   212/852-2130
PFFL American Choral Directors Assn., AGAC, Dramatists Guild; **AFFL** B.A. Swarthmore College, M.M. University of Illinois; **LANG** E, F, G, GK, I, S; **DAYS** Mon. & Thurs., evenings & weekends; **LENG** 1 hr; **COST** $20; **INIT** N; **ACMP** Self; **NEWS** Y; **PERF** Referral to directors, conductors, composers for parts in shows; **EDEX** Conductor of over 50 musicals, revues, operas & nightclub acts. Extensive work in clubs & studios as singer/songwriter & side man.
COMM Vocal coaching, audition preparation, arranging, musical direction for clubs & cabarets, music theory & sightsinging. I try to structure lessons to needs of individual, incorporating study of music if necessary.

NAME CLINE, EUGENE
ADDR 2109 Broadway, New York, NY 10023   212/873-3629
LANG E, F, G, I; **DAYS** 7 days, including evenings & weekends; **LENG** ½ or 1 hr; **COST** $25/hr; **INIT** N; **ACMP** Self; **NEWS** Y; **PERF** N; **FAME** Donnie Rae Albert, Donald George, Kenneth Shaw; **EDEX** M.A. Piano Accompanying—University of Missouri, Kansas City; former assistant conductor—Kansas City Lyric Theatre & New Orleans Opera.

NAME COGLEY, MARK
ADDR 166 W. 76th Street, #4-A, New York, NY 10023   212/595-6914
PFFL Assistant chorus master—Metropolitan Opera; **AFFL** Opera Association, Oberlin College; **LANG** E, F, G, I, R; **DAYS** Mon.–Sat. & evenings; **LENG** 1 hr; **COST** $20; **INIT** N; **ACMP** Self; **NEWS** Y; **EDEX** Vocal coach—Music Academy of the West ('75–'76), University of Wisc./Milwaukee ('77–'78), Met Opera ('79–   ). Supervised L. Bernstein's N.Y. workshop of new *A Quiet Place*.
COMM Have a general familiarity with vocal repertoire—song, oratorio, opera—& my sight-reading ability makes it possible for me to assimilate quickly what singer is apt to bring in.

NAME DORNEMANN, JOAN***
ADDR 170 W. 73rd Street, #7-A 1, New York, NY 10023   212/362-5980

PFFL Assistant conductor—Metropolitan Opera; **AFFL** Master class teacher at the AIMS Summer Vocal Institute, Graz, Austria; **LANG** E, I, F, S.

NAME   EDWARDS, LEILA***
ADDR   162 W. 54th Street, New York, NY 10019   212/247-3287

PFFL NYSTA, American Theatre Wing; **AFFL** Hunter College; **DAYS** Mon.–Sat. including evenings; **LENG** 1 hr; **COST** $20; **INIT** N; **ACMP** Self; **NEWS** Y; **FAME** Sherrill Milnes, Justino Diaz, Licia Albanese, Mario Lanza, Kurt Baum; **EDEX** B.S. in Ed.—Worcester State College, graduate study at Clarke University. Accompanist & coach for Robert Merrill—7 years, Herva Nelli—15 years, Claramae Turner—15 years. Concerts all over U.S. & Canada through NCAC.

COMM Other famous students: Jussi Bjoerling, Susanne Marsee, Cornell MacNeil, Chester Ludgin, Salvatore Baccaloni, Richard Cassilly, Dominic Cossa, Richard Fredricks.

NAME   ELIASEN, MIKAEL
ADDR   235 W. 75th Street, #8-H, New York, NY 10023   212/362-6556

PFFL Musicians Union; **AFFL** Freelance; **LANG** E, F, G, I, SW, D, H; **DAYS** 7 days, evenings & weekends; **LENG** 1 hr; **COST** $30; **INIT** N; **ACMP** Self; **NEWS** Y; **FAME** Robert Merrill, Tom Krause, Theodor Uppman, Donald Gramm, Mira Zakai; **EDEX** McGill Univ.—Lic. Mus., post-graduate studies—Vienna. Recitals in world's major cities. Recitals in U.S.; tours of Orient, Israel, Russia, Australia. Master classes in major universities around world. Recordings.

NAME   GOLDBERG, JEFFREY***
ADDR   40 W. 72nd Street, #31-C, New York, NY 10023   212/362-7323

PFFL San Francisco Opera staff; **LANG** E, F, G, I; **DAYS** Mon.–Fri., days; **LENG** 1 hr; **COST** $25; **INIT** $25; **ACMP** Self; **NEWS** Y; **EDEX** Alumnus of AIMS Summer Vocal Institute in Graz, Austria.

NAME   GORDON, RICHARD
ADDR   409 W. 52nd Street, #4-FW-11, New York, NY 10019   212/974-1052

PFFL AF of M; **AFFL** American Musical & Dramatic Academy; **LANG** E, F, G, I; **DAYS** 7 days, evenings & weekends; **LENG** 1 hr; **COST** $20; **INIT** N; **ACMP** Self; **NEWS** Y; **PERF** Small workshops; **FAME** Patrice Munsel, Jane Powell, Barbara Moore; **EDEX** Indiana University; S.M.U.; conductor for national tours of Broadway musicals; chamber music.

COMM Specialize in French art songs.

NAME GRUBB, THOMAS
ADDR 160 W. 73rd Street, New York, NY 10023   212/877-6700
PFFL Academie Maurice Ravel (France), NATS; **TLOC** 212/787-7965; **AFFL** Faculty, Manhattan School of Music, Academy of Vocal Arts (Philadelphia); **LANG** E, F, G, I, S, L; **DAYS** Days, Mon.–Fri.; **LENG** 1 hr+; **ACMP** Self; **NEWS** Y; **EDEX** M.M. (piano), Manhattan School; M.A. (Fr.), Yale; B.A., Eastman; coaching & accompanying Pierre Bernac; extensive tours as accompanist, North America & Europe; recordings with Lyrachord & Orion; master classes in U.S.A. & France.
COMM Specialties—French for Singers, French Vocal Repertoire, recital pianist–accompanist, recital program planning; adjudicator, Metropolitan Opera Guild Auditions, Concours Internationale de Chant de Paris.

NAME HALL, DONALD R.
ADDR 280 Riverside Drive, #6-L, New York, NY 10025   212/866-5952
AFFL Faculty, Manhattan School of Music; **LANG** F, G, I, R; **DAYS** Mon., Wed., Thurs.; **LENG** 1 hr; **COST** $20; **INIT** N; **ACMP** Self; **NEWS** Y; **FAME** Dolora Yajic—bronze medal Tschaikowsky Competition & other artists; **EDEX** Ph.D. in Modern Languages & Literature from Yale University, professor of German diction at Manhattan School of Music (& Russian for singers at Extension Division). Russian teacher—Maria Kurenko.
COMM Consider self to be vocal coach only & do not touch on voice production. Have studied singing & so am familiar with matters of vocal technique. Deal with matters relating to polished performance.

NAME HOLKEBOER, DAVID
ADDR 2109 Broadway, Apt. 8-157, New York, NY 10023   212/874-1050
PFFL Chamber Opera Theatre of New York; **LANG** E, I, G, F; **DAYS** Mon.–Sat., including evenings; **LENG** ½ or 1 hr; **COST** $20/hr; **INIT** N; **ACMP** Self; **NEWS** Y; **EDEX** M.M. from University of Illinois with John Wustman.

NAME JACKSON, CLIFF***
ADDR 7 E. 124th Street, New York, NY 10035   212/410-0402
PFFL Lake George Opera; **EDEX** Alumnus of AIMS Summer Vocal Institute in Graz, Austria.

NAME KAY, ALBERT
ADDR 58 W. 58th Street, #31E, New York, NY 10019   212/593-1640
PFFL NYSTA, The Bohemians, AGMA; **AFFL** American Theatre Wing, Lan-

guage Teacher 1945–52; **LANG** I, F, G; **DAYS** 7 days, evenings & weekends; **LENG** 55 min; **COST** $25; **INIT** N; **ACMP** $15 per hour; **NEWS** Y; **PERF** Bookings if student is exceptionally talented with potential; **FAME** Alexander Sved, Florence Easton, Richard Tauber, Vera Schwarz; **EDEX** B.A., CCNY; language teacher at American Theatre Wing; official translator—Royal Greek Consulate; taught many of Florence Easton's pupils. Others: Hans Jaray, Frank Loesser, Elena Nikolaidi.

COMM Specialty is teaching singers text of arias, songs & lieder, stressing vocabulary, syntax, grammar, semantics & most of all correct pronunciation & accent.

NAME　KOLODY, JOHN T.***
ADDR　103 2nd Avenue, #2-B, New York, NY 10003　　212/477-3862

AFFL Staff pianist at AIMS Summer Vocal Institute in Graz, Austria; **DAYS** 7 days, evenings & weekends; **COST** $20; **NEWS** Y; **PERF** Small workshops, private recitals, scenes from operas; **FAME** Rosalind Elias, Andrea Velis, Toshiaki Kundi; **EDEX** B.M.—Susquehanna University, M.M.—N.Y.U., studies at Manhattan School of Music, Fordham Univ., AIMS—Graz. Assistant director N.Y.U. Choral Arts Society & accompanist for N.Y. Choral Society.

COMM Lesson lengths are 30 min for voice or 1 hr as coach.

NAME　KUIPERS, JULIE
ADDR　25–04 44th Street, New York, NY 11103　　212/728-0788

TLOC See below; **LANG** E, I, G, F; **DAYS** 7 days; **LENG** ½ or 1 hr; **COST** $15/hr; **INIT** N; **ACMP** Self; **NEWS** Y; **EDEX** M.M. from University of Illinois with John Wustman.

COMM Coaching locations are arranged for singers' convenience.

NAME　LEBOWITZ, MARK
ADDR　414 Amsterdam Avenue, #4-R, New York, NY 10024　212/580-7256

PFFL AFTRA, SAG, AEA; **AFFL** Dartmouth College, Fordham University; **LANG** I, F, G; **DAYS** 7 days, evenings & weekends; **LENG** 1 hr; **COST** $20; **INIT** $20; **ACMP** Self; **NEWS** Y; **PERF** Help with booking of club acts; **EDEX** B.A., Dartmouth College; New England Conservatory.

COMM I accompany singers & coach for auditions & nightclub material, mostly musical theater & popular music. Also accompany & work on classical material. Transcription, transpositions, sight-reading, arrangements.

NAME　LEIGHTON, DAVID
ADDR　170 W. 73rd Street, New York, NY 10023　　212/873-9531

DAYS Tues.–Fri., days only; **ACMP** provided; **NEWS** Y; **PERF** Yes; **EDEX** Assistant conductor, Metropolitan Opera ('73–'81). Extensive conducting & recital tours.

NAME LEWIS, KATHRYN
ADDR 69 Payson Avenue, New York, NY 10034   212/304-0502
AFFL Brooklyn College Conservatory of Music; **LANG** F, I, G; **DAYS** 7, incl. evenings; **LENG** 1 hr; **COST** $15; **INIT** N; **ACMP** Self; **NEWS** Y; **EDEX** B.M. in piano, University of Maryland; M.M. in vocal accompanying & coaching, University of Illinois with John Wustman. Music director, Brunswick Music Theater; staff, Chautauqua Music School, Illinois Opera Theater, Montgomery Village Center for Performing Arts (Maryland).

NAME MALLOY, GEORGE
ADDR 166 W. 72nd Street, New York, NY 10023   212/595-8381
PFFL AFM, NYSTA; **DAYS** Tues.–Sat., evenings & weekends; **LENG** 1 hr; **INIT** N; **NEWS** Y; **FAME** Accompanist for Eileen Farrell, Roberta Peters, Martina Arroyo; **EDEX** Graduate University of Southern California, student of Emanuel Bay & Gwendolyn Koldofsky. Concert tours of U.S.A., Canada, Far East, Europe, Africa, Israel.

NAME MASON, GREGORY
ADDR 25-04 44th Street, #14, Astoria, NY 11103   728-0788
TLOC TBA; **LANG** G, F, I; **DAYS** 7 days; **LENG** 1 hr; **COST** $20; **INIT** N **ACMP** Self; **NEWS** Y; **EDEX** University of Michigan, University of Illinois. Have played with top teachers/contests; accompanied William Warfield; studied with Eugene Bossart & John Wustman.

NAME McASSEY, MICHAEL
ADDR 150 W. 47th Street, #5-A, New York, NY 10036   212/354-8468
PFFL AEA, SAG; **LANG** E; **DAYS** Mon.–Sat., days & evenings; **LENG** 1 hr; **COST** $20; **INIT** $10; **ACMP** Self; **NEWS** Y; **PERF** Recommendations by casting directors—on own as director; **FAME** Nicolette Goulet & Broadway casts of *Annie, Nine, Dreamgirls, Barnum*; **EDEX** Musical Theatre major— Eastern Ill. Univ. Appeared under Hal Prince in *Silverlake, Gay Company, Godspell, I Love My Wife* & numerous stock & regional companies. Musical Director for Center Stage (Baltimore).

COMM O'Neill Theatre, Stonewall Rep., Little Theatre on the Square, S. Jer Regional Theatre. Appear at Don't Tell Mama as pianist/singer & frequently present my club act there.

NAME   NOLD, DONAL
ADDR   124 W. 71st Street, New York, NY 10023   212/787-0196
AFFL Manhattan School of Music, Chairman Accompanying Dept./Vocal Coaching; **LANG** F, G, I, S, R; **DAYS** Tues., Wed., Fri.; **LENG** 1 hr; **INIT** Y; **NEWS** Y; **FAME** Teacher of coaches in opera houses in Zurich, Lucerne, Heidelberg; **EDEX** M.S., Juilliard; piano with Samaroff, Freundlich, Long (Paris). Solo recitals Europe, Latin America, Canada, U.S. & Far East; appearances with Forrester, Bumbry, Arroyo, Diaz. Residence in Europe ten years.
COMM Fees available by calling Mr. Nold personally.

NAME   OBERLIN, RUSSELL
ADDR   Hunter College, 695 Park Ave., New York, NY 10021   212/570-5736
PFFL N.Y.C. Chapter Board Member of NATS; **AFFL** City University of N.Y.: Hunter College & Graduate Center; **DAYS** Tues. & Fri., days only; **LENG** 1 hr; **COST** $50; **INIT** $50; **NEWS** Y
COMM Full-time professor of music at Hunter College. In addition, gives limited number of private coaching sessions in repertoire and performance.

NAME   PENN, ELAINE***
ADDR   365 West End Avenue, #9-D, New York, NY 10024   212/874-6506
AFFL Vocal coach at AIMS Summer Vocal Institute in Graz, Austria

NAME   POPPER, FREDRIC
ADDR   84-10 143rd Street, Jamaica, NY 11435   212/658-6218
PFFL Goldovsky Opera Theatre; **AFFL** Curtis Institute, Philadelphia; Mannes College of Music, N.Y.C.; **LANG** E, F, G, GK, H, I, S; **DAYS** Evenings & weekends; **LENG** 1 hr; **COST** $30; **INIT** N; **NEWS** Y

NAME   POSELL, GEORGE***
ADDR   465 West End Avenue, New York, NY 10024   212/362-6093
PFFL Metropolitan Opera, San Francisco Opera; **LANG** E, F, G, I, R, S; **DAYS** Mon.–Sat., & evenings; **LENG** 1 hr; **COST** $45; **INIT** $30; **ACMP** Self; **NEWS** Y; **FAME** Leontyne Price, Renata Scotto, Placido Domingo, Grace Bumbry; **EDEX** M.M., Indiana Univ.; Met Opera, San Francisco Opera, Chicago Lyric, Santa Fe, Lake George, Cleveland Opera, Australian Opera, Royal Opera-Stockholm, Finnish National Opera, Basler Staattheater, Madrid Festival.
COMM Specialties—German and contemporary literature. Former faculty member of AIMS Summer Vocal Institute in Graz, Austria. Highly recommended.

NAME POWELL, R. STEWART
ADDR 436 W. Broadway, New York, NY 10012   212/925-5131
PFFL NYSTA; **DAYS** Mon.–Sat., days & evenings; **LENG** 1 hr; **COST** $20;
INIT N; **NEWS** Y; **EDEX** A.B., University of North Carolina; M.S. in Piano—
Juilliard School; Royal Conservatory of Mons, Belgium. Performed throughout
Europe & U.S.

NAME RICCIARDONE, MICHAEL
ADDR 305 W. 45th Street, #5-E, New York, NY 10036   212/307-0996

NAME RICH, MARTIN***
ADDR 57 W. 58th Street, #6-A, New York, NY 10019   212/753-2286
PFFL Former conductor, Metropolitan Opera; **AFFL** Faculty, AIMS Summer
Vocal Institute in Graz, Austria; **LANG** E, I, F, G; **LENG** 45 min; **COST** $40;
INIT Y; **ACMP** Y; **NEWS** Y; **EDEX** For more than 20 years a leading coach &
conductor at Metropolitan Opera. Has accompanied some of most famous
singers of generation, including Tebaldi and Siepi.
COMM Highly recommended. On Tuesdays teaches at 1922 Spruce Street,
Philadelphia, PA; 215/545-1111.

NAME SHEPPARD, MERYL
ADDR 140 W. 69th Street, New York, NY 10023   212/541-7600
PFFL AGVA, BMI; **LANG** E, F, S; **DAYS** Mon.–Sat., days & evenings; **LENG**
1 hr; **COST** $25; **INIT** N; **ACMP** Self; **NEWS** Y; **EDEX** Manhattan School of
Music, Oberlin—B.M. Music Education. Perform in nightclubs all over N.Y.C.
and L.A.
COMM Do studio work in pop rock/blues genre, coach & teach voice. Can
teach students to sing in one introductory lesson & help them realize their
power.

NAME SILVER, JACQUELYNE
ADDR 155 W. 68th Street, New York, NY 10023   212/496-7104
PFFL AFM Local 802; **LANG** E, F, I; **DAYS** Mon.–Sat., evenings & weekends;
LENG 1 hr; **COST** $45; **INIT** $45; **ACMP** Self; **NEWS** Y; **FAME** Marilyn Horne,
Tony Randall, John Cullum, Ron Holgate, Maralin Niska; **EDEX** Juilliard School,
master classes at leading universities in U.S.

NAME SONNTAG, STANLEY***
ADDR 160 W. 73rd Street, New York, NY 10023   212/873-2350

PFFL NYSTA, NATS, AMC, AFM Local 802; **AFFL** Manhattanville College, SUNY at Purchase; **LANG** G, F, I, E; **DAYS** Tues.–Wed., Purchase; other, studio; **LENG** 1 hr; **COST** $20; **INIT** N; **ACMP** Self; **NEWS** Y; **FAME** Kenneth Riegel, Rosalind Elias, Teresa Stratas, Martina Arroyo, Arlene Saunders; **EDEX** Master of Arts in Education—NYU. Thirty years' recital experience.

COMM Co-author of book *The Art of the Song Recital* (Schirmer). Authority on recital performance. Have performed master classes & workshops in many universities & colleges.

NAME   SPERRY, PAUL
ADDR   115 Central Park West, New York, NY 10023   212/595-3020

PFFL NATS; **AFFL** Aspen Music Festival; **LANG** E, F, G, I; **DAYS** Occasional weekends; **LENG** 1 hr; **COST** $40; **INIT** N; **ACMP** You provide; **NEWS** Y; **EDEX** Given concerts throughout U.S. & Europe. Perform recitals, oratorio & contemporary music, occasionally opera.

COMM Have a large repertoire of songs in many languages & am an enthusiast for American songs. Have taught master classes & workshops in colleges, conservatories & universities across country.

NAME   STEPHAN, PAUL N.
ADDR   114 Nagle Avenue, #4-C, New York, NY 10040   212/942-9189

PFFL Kappa Gamma Psi; **LANG** E, F, G, I; **DAYS** Mon.–Sat. including evenings; **LENG** ½ or 1 hr; **COST** $25/hr; **INIT** N; **ACMP** Self; **NEWS** Y; **PERF** In studio master class; **EDEX** B.M. (Voice)—Ithaca College, M.F.A.—University of Utah. Teachers include Lowell & Naomi Farr, E. Leslie Bennett, Richard White, Mary Ann Covert, Hans Boepple, Amy McGrath, & D. Davidson Hauskee.

NAME   STRASFOGEL, IGNACE
ADDR   30 Lincoln Plaza, New York, NY 10023   212/799-3100

PFFL Conductor and coach, Metropolitan Opera; **LANG** E, F, G, I; **DAYS** By appointment only—no evenings; **LENG** 1 hr; **COST** $40; **INIT** $40; **ACMP** Self; **NEWS** Y; **PERF** Indirectly; **FAME** See *Who's Who in Music*

COMM If you wish to coach, please send letter & include resume & curriculum vitae. Methods taught: artistic projection & interpretation, & opera & lied coaching.

NAME   TOSCANI, SMARANDA
ADDR   33-22 83rd Street, Jackson Heights, NY 11372   212/592-5161

TLOC New York City; **AFFL** Ciprian Porumbescu Musical Conservatory, Bucharest, Romania; **LANG** E, F, I, Romanian; **DAYS** Evenings & weekends; **LENG** 1 hr; **COST** $20; **INIT** $20; **ACMP** Self; **NEWS** Y; **EDEX** Voice with Dumitru Toscani. Was piano coach at conservatory for opera productions at National Romanian Theater. Sang with Romanian National Opera, held concerts of art songs & lied at Romanian National Radio & TV.

COMM Operatic repertory: *Rigoletto* — Gilda; *Lucia di Lammermoor* — Lucia; *Il Barbiere di Siviglia* — Rosina.

NAME   TRIESTRAM, DAVID
ADDR   201 W. 70th Street, New York, NY 10023   212/724-8779

PFFL Santa Fe Opera music staff; **LANG** F, I, G; **DAYS** Mon. – Sat., 10 – 7 P.M.; **LENG** 1 hr; **COST** Inquire; **ACMP** Self; **NEWS** Y; **EDEX** B.M., Oberlin College; private study in Boston with John Moriarty.

COMM Specialize in lieder & opera. Available for auditions.

NAME   VAN BUSKIRK, JOHN
ADDR   945 West End Avenue, New York, NY 10025   212/316-1822

LANG E, I, F, G; **DAYS** Mon. – Sat.; **LENG** 1 hr; **COST** Inquire; **INIT** Y; **ACMP** Self; **NEWS** Y; **EDEX** B.M., Eastman School of Music; M.M., Juilliard School. Further studies at Liszt Academy, Budapest. Extensive solo, accompanying & chamber music performances.

COMM Specialize in songs & lieder.

NAME   WALLACE, ROBERT***
ADDR   235 W. 102nd Street, #12-U, New York, NY 10025   212/316-3196

PFFL National Opera Assn, COS, AFM Local 802; **AFFL** Guest lecturer: Clarion State, Lou. Tech. Univ., S. Ill. Univ., SUNY-Pur, E. Texas State; **LANG** E, F, G, I, S; **DAYS** Mon. – Sat., days & evenings; **LENG** 1 hr; **COST** $25; **ACMP** Self; **NEWS** Y; **PERF** Recommendations for operas, recitals and churches; **FAME** Douglas Ahlstedt, Spiro Malas, Louis Quilico, Charles Long, Nicola Ghiuselev; **EDEX** B.M. (Piano), Manhattan School of Music, M.M. (Piano), Manhattan; operatic seminars with George Schick, Boris Goldovsky.

COMM Conducted with several opera companies. Coach — Chautauqua, N.Y.C. Opera, Metropolitan Opera Studio, San Francisco Merola Program, Opera Metropolitana of Caracas, New Orleans Opera. Solo recitals, U.S. & Europe.

NAME   WALSER, LLOYD ALAN
ADDR   200 W. 70th Street, #3-G, New York, NY 10023   212/799-6801

PFFL New York City Opera; **LANG** E, F, G, I; **DAYS** Mon.—Sat., evenings & weekends; **LENG** 1 hr; **COST** $30; **INIT** N; **ACMP** Self; **NEWS** Y; **FAME** Maralin Niska, Diane Curry, Alexandra Hunt, Susanne Marsee; **EDEX** University of Oklahoma, University of Texas, Yale University, Fulbright scholar to Rome. Conducted with N.Y.C. Opera, Cultural Center of Philippine Philharmonic Orchestra.

COMM Specialties—vocal instruction & repertoire coaching

NAME   WAXMAN, BOB
ADDR   28 Orchid Drive, Port Jefferson Station, NY 11776   516/928-2855

PFFL NYSTA, Theater Directors Guild, Players Club of Metropolitan Life; **TLOC** Port Jefferson Station & NYC; **LANG** I, F; **DAYS** Mon.—Fri. including evenings; **LENG** 1 hr; **COST** $25; **INIT** $25; **ACMP** Self; **NEWS** Y; **PERF** Private auditions with managers, cabarets, clubs & Broadway theater; **FAME** Swenson, Kitt, Rivers, Streisand, Hamilton, Francis, Davidson; **EDEX** New School of Music—Philadelphia, Peabody Conservatory, Carnegie Tech.; director of Broadway, off Broadway, regional theaters; executive director of Players Club.

COMM Coach singers, prepare repertoire, direct them in stage technique & auditions. Am moving out of N.Y.C. but will teach there as well. Studio phone in N.Y. will be 212/243-0597.

NAME   WEINRICH, CYNTHIA
ADDR   180 Claremont Avenue, New York, NY 10027   212/663-0571

PFFL NATS, AGO; **TLOC** Above and in Hoboken, N.J.; **LANG** E, F, G, I, R; **DAYS** Varied; evenings & weekends; **LENG** 45—60 min; **COST** $20; **INIT** $20 **ACMP** Provided—$6/hr; **NEWS** Y; **PERF** Small workshops, guidance in performing at different levels; **EDEX** M.M.—New England Conservatory, formerly vocal coach at Harvard University. Performer in recital, opera, operetta, stage; studies with Gladys Miller, Susan Clickner; coached with Peter Pears, Olga Averino, Janet Bookspan.

COMM Vocal technique & repertoire (song & opera) coaching; diction for speech & singing.

NAME   WOITACH, RICHARD
ADDR   697 West End Avenue, New York, NY 10025   212/799-3100

PFFL Conductor and coach, Metropolitan Opera; **LANG** E, F, G, I; **DAYS** Varied, & evenings; **LENG** 45 min; **COST** $60; **INIT** N; **ACMP** Self; **FAME** Teresa Stratas, Regina Resnik

NAME ZUCKER, STEFAN
ADDR 11 Riverside Drive, New York, NY 10023   212/877-1595

PFFL Assoc. for the Furtherment of Bel Canto, AFBC Records, WKCR-FM; **LANG** E, F, G, I, S; **DAYS** 7 days, evenings & weekends; **LENG** 1 hr; **COST** $30; **INIT** $30; **ACMP** Provided; **NEWS** Y; **PERF** Radio appearances, recordings, major concert hall performances; **EDEX** Juilliard, Hartt, Mozarteum, New England Conservatory, Columbia University; N.Y. Univ. Performed at Fisher, Town and Merkin concert halls; on radio & TV. Contributor to *Am. Record Guide, Opera News, N.Y. Herald Tribune.*

COMM Specialty—bel canto repertory. Help students eliminate random & misplaced accents, prepare climax points with well-developed upbeats & taper resolutions of dissonances. Specialize in Italian & German.

Each of the teachers in the following list was sent a questionnaire requesting the information in the code. As much of the supplied information as possible appears in each entry. We have marked with three asterisks (***) the teachers whom we at AIMS have worked with and know to be effective.

Code

NAME   Professional name

ADDR   Current address and telephone number

PFFL   Professional affiliations, including unions, learned societies and/ or positions with professional companies

TLOC   Teaching location if different from address above

DAYS   Days when teaches

AFFL   Academic affiliations, including colleges and institutes where currently teaching

LENG   Length of lesson

COST   Cost of lesson

INIT   Is there a consultation or initial audition fee?
(Y = yes, N = no)

ACMP   Is accompanist provided, and if so, is there an additional fee?

NEWS   Are new students being accepted?

PERF   Are performing opportunities provided?

FAME   Famous or well-known students

EDEX   Educational background and performing experience of teacher

COMM   Comments

NAME AINSBERG, EDITH GORDON
ADDR 4525 Henry Hudson Parkway, Riverdale, NY 10471 212/549-6408
PFFL NYSTA, Board of Governors of American Society of Jewish Music; **TLOC** 92nd Street Y (and home); **DAYS** Tues.–Sat., days; **AFFL** Voice teacher at 92nd Street Y Music School; **LENG** 45 min; **COST** $35; **INIT** N; **ACMP** Y; **NEWS** Y; **PERF** Student recitals at YMHA Music School; **FAME** Viola Harris, Susan Karpman, Beverly Rich; **EDEX** Graduate of Juilliard.

Soloist, Paris Opera Ballet, Tanglewood, BSO, Cleveland Pops, Little Orchestra Society, Goldovsky Opera Theatre, St. Paul Civic Opera, Chautauqua. TV appearances on CBS, NBC.

COMM Recorded on Mercury, Tikva & most recently was soloist in Kurt Weill's *Frauentanz* on Leonarda label; soprano soloist for last ten years with Bronx Arts Ensemble; starred in *The Telephone* on Broadway & national tour.

NAME ALESSANDRO, LENORE
ADDR 2109 Broadway, Studio 1379, New York, NY 10023   212/799-7280
PFFL NYSTA; **DAYS** Mon.–Sat., including evenings & weekends; **LENG** 45–60 min; **COST** $40; **INIT** N; **ACMP** Y—$10; **NEWS** Y; **PERF** Once a year, opera photo shots of pupils in opera scenes available; **FAME** Christopher Collins, Greg Mitchell, Sheila Shumate, Arlene Adler; **EDEX** Taught vocal music in high school. Studied with Zenatello, Coradetta, Liebling, Tetrazzini & other famous teachers. New York recital with Paul Ulanovsky at Carnegie Hall, 1956.

COMM Programs of authentication shown on request.

NAME ALEXANDER, ELLEN***
ADDR 365 West End Avenue, #9D, New York, NY 10024   212/874-6506
PFFL AFTRA, Equity, AGMA; **AFFL** Faculty member of AIMS Summer Vocal Institute in Graz, Austria; Marymount College; **LENG** 1 hr; **COST** $40; **ACMP** Y, no fee; **PERF** 4–6 concerts per year, language master class, stage presentation classes; **EDEX** Graduate P.C.P.A., Temple University, studied with E. Giannini Gregory (Curtis Institute, pupil of Marcella Sembrich), Margarete Matzenauer, George London. N.Y.C. Opera, G&S, Little Orchestra Society, Philadelphia Orchestra, Chicago Symphony, Goodspeed Opera, Concert Artists Guild award winner.

COMM St. Bartholomew's soloist for 14 years. Current soloist at St. Patrick's Cathedral.

NAME AMES, PERRY, STUDIO OF VOCAL ARTS
ADDR 640 Fulton Street, Rt. 109, Farmingdale, NY 11735   212/249-3940
PFFL NATS, MENC, NYSTA, NMEA, Mu Phi Epsilon; **DAYS** Mon.–Sat., evenings & weekends; **LENG** Varies; **INIT** Y; **ACMP** Y; **NEWS** Y; **PERF** Variety show & concerts in suitable hall or night club; **FAME** Foreigner, Thrills, Johnny Nash, Bobby Darin, Tommy Eioneete, Spys; **EDEX** 30 years' experience in night clubs in U.S. & Europe. Graduate of Music Conservatory.

COMM Like to think of self & staff as dedicated professionals who strive for perfection in training students. Don't be afraid to check a voice teacher's credentials. It's your voice, so protect it.

NAME ANDREAS, THEODORA
ADDR 410 Benedict Avenue, Apt. 1-C, Tarrytown, NY 10591   212/787-8964
PFFL AGMA, AEA, NYSTA, Schubert Club; **TLOC** 2109 Broadway, #13-92, 212/870-5249; **DAYS** Mon.–Fri., including evenings; **AFFL** University of Minnesota Alumni Association; **LENG** 1 hr; **COST** $35; **INIT** Y; **ACMP** Y; **NEWS** Y; **PERF** In process of forming masterwork workshop; **FAME** M. Henderson, D. Bullock, S. Santiago, N. Flacks, K. Mars, T. Hernandez; **EDEX** Graduate of University of Minnesota & Juilliard. Studies in piano. Major roles with New York City Opera, Pittsburgh Opera, Cincinnati Opera, St. Paul. Concerts in Rome, New York. St. Paul Chamber Orchestra, CBS.
COMM Past winner of Metropolitan Opera Upper-Midwest Regional Auditions

NAME ANSELMO, ANDY THOMAS
ADDR The Singers Forum, 137 Fifth Ave., New York, NY 10010 212/989-4248
PFFL Equity, AGVA, NYSTA, Players Club; **DAYS** Mon.–Fri., including evenings; **AFFL** Lee Strasberg Institute; **LENG** 30 min; **COST** $40; **INIT** $50; **ACMP** Y; **NEWS** Y; **PERF** Cabaret shows, operas, musical comedy scenes, microphone technique; **FAME** Brooke Shields, Mary Tyler Moore, Joanne Woodward, Mia Farrow; **EDEX** Vocal Director of *Agnes of God;* leads in Broadway shows; performed *Most Happy Fellow* with many opera companies in New York, Las Vegas & Hollywood on tour in major hotels & nightclubs.

NAME ANTHONY, CLARISSA
ADDR 8 Waterbury Road, Upper Montclair, NJ 07043   201/746-4751
PFFL NYSTA, Montclair Music Club, NATS, The Rehearsal Club, Phi Beta; **TLOC** Wayne and Upper Montclair, NJ; **DAYS** Mon.–Sat., including weekends; **AFFL** Wm. Paterson College, Wayne, NJ; **LENG** 1 hr; **COST** $20; **INIT** N; **ACMP** Y; **NEWS** Y; **EDEX** M.M. in Voice, University of Oregon; B.A. in Voice; finalist for San Francisco Opera Finals, participant in Merola Opera Theatre; soloist Temple Emanu-El, New York City.

NAME ARCAYA, BERET
ADDR 10 White Street, New York, NY 10013   212/226-2359

NAME BAIRD, ROBERT G.
ADDR 171 W. 71st Street, New York, NY 10023   212/362-4848
PFFL NYSTA, NATS; **DAYS** Mon., Tues., Fri., Sat.; **LENG** 30 min.; **COST** $25; **INIT** $25; **ACMP** N; **NEWS** Y; **FAME** William Olvis, Moritz Stern, Vernon Shinall, Ray Bolger; **EDEX** Pupil of William C. Fry, Rose Dirman, Cornelius Reid, Douglas Stanley, Leon Rothier & Paul Althouse. American Theatre Wing Professional Training Program, Amato Opera (1950–).

NAME BARLOW, KLARA
ADDR 60 W. 57th Street, New York, NY 10019   212/765-0983
PFFL AGMA, NYSTA, Equity, Metropolitan Opera; **TLOC** Home and studios; **DAYS** Flexible, including evenings; **AFFL** Master classes at Montclair State J. Hines Newark Arts Center; **LENG** 1 hr; **COST** $50; **INIT** $60; **ACMP** Y; **NEWS** Y; **PERF** Agent contacts, private recitals, workshops; **EDEX** Hamburg, Vienna, Munich, LaScala, West Berlin, East Berlin, Dresden, Stuttgart, Zurich. German, French, Italian regional opera. Active national, international & regional companies; Canadian opera; TV & films.
COMM Teaches acting-motivation-characterization personality development, traditional staging of opera roles. Worked with stage directors Rennert, Everding, Strehler, Felsenstein. Judge for Dealey Competition, Dallas.

NAME BARON, CARMEN
ADDR 98 Bayview Avenue, Northport, NY 11768   516/757-6433
PFFL NATS, AFTRA; **DAYS** Mon. – Thurs. & Sat., including evenings; **LENG** 45 min; **COST** $18; **INIT** Y; **ACMP** N; **NEWS** Y; **PERF** Small workshops; **EDEX** Voice major at Juilliard; voice production major, Hofstra University. Teaches Oren Brown Method. Studied with Elda Eicale, Paul Althouse, Shirley Meir & Thomas Houser.

NAME BAYARD, CAROL
ADDR 400 W. 43rd Street, New York, NY 10036   212/279-3054
PFFL AGMA; **DAYS** Mon. – Sat.; **LENG** 1 hr; **COST** $40; **INIT** $40; **ACMP** Y; **NEWS** Y; **EDEX** Leading soprano with N.Y.C. Opera for ten years, performing Manon, Marguerite, Rosalinda, Countess, Nedda, etc. Performed with most of major U.S. opera companies. World premiere of Curley's Wife in *Of Mice and Men.*

NAME BOYAJIAN, ARMEN
ADDR 825 West End Avenue, Apt. 3-B, New York, NY 10025 212/666-2678
TLOC NYC & Paterson, NJ 201/523-7904; **DAYS** Mon. – Sat., 1–5 P.M.; **AFFL** Juilliard School; Montclair State Teachers College; **LENG** 1 hr; **COST** $50; **INIT** $50; **ACMP** N; **NEWS** N; **PERF** Recommendations to agents, conductors & impresarios; **FAME** Paul Plishka, Samuel Ramey, Lili Chookasian, Mignon Dunn, Rosalind Elias, Marisa Galvany, Gwynn Cornell, Harry Theyard, Enrico di Giuseppe, Dominic Cossa, Jean Kraft, Shirley Love, Teresa Kubiak, Chester Ludgin, J. Patrick Raftery; **EDEX** Piano soloist with North Jersey Philharmonic & Symphony Orchestra of Englewood; founder & artistic director of Paterson Lyric Opera Theatre; accompanist to above artists & Beverly Sills (1955–56).

NAME BRADLEY, BONNIE
ADDR 123 W. 57th Street, New York, NY 10019   212/942-4967
PFFL AGMA, NYAG, NATS, College Music Society; **DAYS** Mon.–Sat., including evenings; **LENG** 1 hr; **COST** $30; **INIT** $30; **ACMP** N; **NEWS** Y; **EDEX** M.M., Opera Performance from Manhattan School. European experience. Soloist, N.Y. Philharmonic, American Symphony, Princeton Chamber Orchestra, Aldeburgh Festival, Salzburg Festival, Santa Fe, Metropolitan Opera Studio.
COMM Oratorio Society of New York, New York Choral Society; *Who's Who of Outstanding American Women 1983.*

NAME BROWN, OREN L.
ADDR 160 W. 73rd Street, New York, NY 10023   212/873-8269
PFFL NATS, NYSTA, FAERS; **DAYS** Mon., Wed., Fri.—days only; **AFFL** Juilliard School; **LENG** ½ or 1 hr; **COST** $60; **INIT** Y; **ACMP** Y; **NEWS** Y; **PERF** Small workshops, private recitals, Brown Voice Seminar, Amherst College; **FAME** Judith Blegen, Ben Holt, Richard McKee, Noelle Rogers, James King, Olivia Stapp, Lenus Carlson, Elizabeth Pruet, John Aler, Henry Price, Sandra Walker, Peter Lightfoot, Jon Humphrey, Judith Haddon, Irene Gubrud; **EDEX** B.M., M.A., Boston University.

NAME BUTIU, SARA
ADDR 91-20 50th Avenue, Elmhurst, NY 11373   212/592-6151
DAYS 7 days, including evenings; **LENG** 1 hr; **COST** $35; **INIT** N; **ACMP** $15/hr extra; **NEWS** Y; **EDEX** Studied in Italy with Victoria Cortez, Stella Simonetti & Emilio Marinesco; in America with Stella Roman; performed in Italy, Romania & Bulgaria.

NAME CAPLAN, JOAN
ADDR 220 E. 73rd Street, New York, NY 10021   212/988-5032
DAYS Tues.-Fri., days only; **LENG** 1 hr; **INIT** N; **ACMP** Y

NAME CARELLI, GABOR P.
ADDR 23 W. 73rd Street, New York, NY 10023   212/874-7454
PFFL AGMA; **DAYS** Mon.–Fri.; **AFFL** Manhattan School of Music; **LENG** ½ or 1 hr; **COST** $45; **INIT** N; **ACMP** Y; **NEWS** Y; **PERF** Auditions; **EDEX** Academy Franz Liszt, Budapest; studies with Gigli in Rome; 23 years as tenor soloist at Metropolitan Opera; soloist & recordings under Toscanini, Dorati, Leinsdorf, Fricsay.

COMM Teaches repertoire in Hungarian, German, Italian, French & English. Teaches opera practicum at Manhattan School.

NAME CASEI, NEDDA
ADDR 15 W. 72nd Street, New York, NY 10023   212/787-3425
PFFL Metropolitan Opera, AGMA, AEA, NATS, Alpha Sigma Lambda; **DAYS** Varies; **LENG** 1 hr+; **COST** $50; **INIT** Y; **ACMP** Extra charge; **NEWS** Y; **PERF** Make suggestions to those I think could use talents of student; **EDEX** Studied voice with Loretta Corelli, William P. Herman, Vittorio Piccinini. Performed at Metropolitan Opera for 18 seasons & in most of world's leading theaters. Judge Metropolitan Opera Auditions.
COMM Fulbright auditions; Norman Treigle Scholarship Contest; master classes at many universities in U.S. & in Hong Kong, Singapore.

NAME CHELSI, LAWRENCE
ADDR 17 Park Avenue, New York, NY 10016   212/689-4596
PFFL NYSTA, NATS, BMI, SAG, AEA, AFTRA; **DAYS** Tues.–Sat.; **AFFL** N.Y.U., Little Theatre Schools; **LENG** 1 hr; **COST** $20; **INIT** N **ACMP** Y; **NEWS** Y; **EDEX** Ten years of piano & voice; studies at Juilliard, Columbia, UCLA, University of Oregon; private study with Gauthier, Singher, De Luca, Martinelli; opera, oratorio, concert, TV, Broadway, commercials, films.
COMM Recordings on RCA, London, Magic-Tone, Rondo. Newcomers to New York City need all the help they can get. It's even tougher now than before, but determination, talent & perseverance still pay off.

NAME CLUTHE, BETTY ANN
ADDR 12 Rolling Hill Drive, Morristown, NJ 07960   201/538-9010
PFFL AEA, AGVA, AFTRA; **DAYS** Mon.–Thurs., days only; **AFFL** Voice faculty at College of St. Elizabeth, Convent Station, NJ; **LENG** 1 hr; **COST** $25; **INIT** N; **ACMP** N; **NEWS** Y; **PERF** MacDowell Club Young Artist Program and small workshops; **EDEX** Juilliard School, Paper Mill Playhouse, recital tours of South America & Scandinavia. Operettas, Broadway shows, oratorios, TV, church soloist.

NAME COLLYER, DAVID SORIN
ADDR 50 W. 67th Street, New York, NY 10023   212/362-2225
PFFL NYSTA, NATS, AEA, AGMA, AFTRA, SAG, AGVA; **DAYS** Will teach evenings; **LENG** 30 min; **COST** $50; **INIT** Y; **ACMP** Y; **NEWS** Y; **PERF** Showcases; **FAME** Liza Minelli, Bette Midler, Paul Simon, Phoebe Snow,

Mellissa Manchester, Colleen Zenk, Leslie Miller; **EDEX** Broadway musicals, opera, concert, night clubs, plays, stock & oratorio.

COMM Teach in various fields—opera, concert, musical comedy, jingle singers, rock singers. We run broad spectrum, speech & diction.

NAME   COSSA, DOMINIC***
ADDR   429 Hegi Drive, New Milford, NJ 07646   201/265-7717
PFFL AGMA, AFTRA, DO, Can. Equity; New York City, Metropolitan, San Francisco operas; **TLOC** NYC (and New Milford); **DAYS** 7, including weekends; **AFFL** Voice instructor, Montclair State College, NJ; **LENG** 1 hr; **COST** $40; **INIT** N; **ACMP** Y; **NEWS** Y; **EDEX** B.S., M.A., Doctor of Humane Letters; 25 years as leading baritone.

NAME   CULTICE, THOMAS G.
ADDR   160 W. 73rd Street, New York, NY 10023   212/799-5503
PFFL NATS, NYSTA; **DAYS** Mon.–Sat.; **LENG** ½ or 1 hr; **COST** TBA; **INIT** Y; **ACMP** Self; **NEWS** Y; **PERF** Studio recitals; **FAME** Richard Evans, Delores Jones, John La Pierre; **EDEX** B.M., University of Michigan; M.M., Indiana University. Studied with Oren Brown, Margaret Harshaw, Paul Matthen, Richard Miller, Frederick Wilkerson. Recitals, opera, oratorio, musical theater throughout U.S.
COMM Particular attention is paid to proper voice classification.

NAME   DAVIS, EUGENE
ADDR   169 W. 88th Street, New York, NY 10024   212/477-9524
PFFL AEA, NATS, MENC, CMS, NAIS, ATIS; **TLOC** 222 E. 16th Street, New York, NY 10003 (724-5480); **DAYS** Mon., Tues., Thurs. & evenings; **AFFL** University of Maine, Auburn University, Friends Seminary; **LENG** 1 hr; **COST** $30; **INIT** N; **ACMP** N; **NEWS** Y; **PERF** Small workshops, private recitals; **EDEX** B.M. & M.M., Indiana University. Two years with Richard Rodgers, Music Theater of Lincoln Center; Green's Gilbert & Sullivan Company; summer theaters including Berkshire Theater Festival, Melody Fair, Carousel Theater.
COMM Available as choral conductor.

NAME   DECATUR, DOUGLAS
ADDR   127 W. 82nd Street, Apt. 3-B, New York, NY 10024   212/873-1880
PFFL NATS; **DAYS** Mon., Tues., Thurs., Fri.—days only; **LENG** 1 hr; **COST** $30; **INIT** Y; **ACMP** $10/hr; **NEWS** Y; **EDEX** North Carolina School of the Arts; Academia Musicale Chigiana, Siena; Instituto di Musica, Rinaldo Franci,

Siena. Teachers: Rose Bampton, Gino Bechi, Giancarlo Montanaro, Norman Farrow, Marlena Malas, Uta Graf, Harvey Woodruff. International Opera Center in Zurich, Joy in Singing Award.

COMM Also coaches singers in Italian in regards to preparing roles.

NAME DELMAN, DITA
ADDR 363 W. South Orange Avenue, South Orange, NJ 07029 201/763-7969
PFFL NATS; Artistic Director, State Repertory Opera; **DAYS** 7, including evenings; **AFFL** Master classes, Brandeis Univ. Extension & South Orange Maplewood Sc.; **LENG** 1 hr; **COST** $35; **INIT** N; **ACMP** Y; **NEWS** Y; **PERF** Private recitals, small roles in State Repertory Opera; **EDEX** B.A., Rutgers University; study with Alberta Masiello, Ignace Strasfogel; performance in opera, concert, oratorio & churches on East Coast.

COMM Voice production concerned with deep abdominal breathing, head resonance & no so-called register change.

NAME DI VIRGILIO, NICHOLAS
ADDR 310 W. 47th Street, Apt. 2-C, New York, NY 10036   212/245-3972
PFFL AGMA, NATS; **DAYS** Thurs.–Sat.; **AFFL** University of Illinois; **LENG** 1 hr; **COST** $50; **INIT** N; **ACMP** $8–10/hr; **NEWS** Y; **EDEX** Graduate of Eastman; Metropolitan Opera, New York City Opera, San Francisco, San Diego, Houston, Miami, Seattle operas; European debut, Brussels.

COMM Premiere of Britten's *War Requiem* at Tanglewood. Professor at University of Illinois; master classes in voice & opera; occasional stage directing.

NAME DOUGLAS, JAN ERIC
ADDR 777 West End Avenue, Apt. 8-A, New York, NY 10025   212/666-1166
PFFL NATS, NYSTA, Voice Foundation; **DAYS** Mon.–Fri.; **AFFL** Faculty, William Paterson College, Wayne, NJ; **LENG** 30 min; **COST** $20; **INIT** $20; **NEWS** Y; **EDEX** D.M., Florida State University. Appeared with Bel Canto Opera, Goldovsky, Atlanta, Gulf Coast Opera Association. Studied voice & pedagogy with Cornelius Reid; soloist First Presbyterian Church, New York City.

COMM Current methods of vocal instruction deal with vocalise & which exercise registers both independently & conjunctively. More attention given to technique than repertoire.

NAME DWYER, DR. EDWARD J.
ADDR 135 W. 69th Street, New York, NY 10023   212/724-1321

DAYS Mon.–Fri., including evenings; **AFFL** Teachers College, Columbia University; **LENG** 45 min; **COST** $60; **INIT** $100; **ACMP** Y; **NEWS** Y; **PERF** Private recitals

COMM Author of book *Singers in New York.*

NAME   EIKENBERRY, E. RICHARD
ADDR   213 Bennett Avenue, Apt. 1-F, New York, NY 10040   212/942-9771
PFFL N.Y.U., Lighthouse for Blind, Bronx Music School; **DAYS** Mon. evening; Fri. all day; **LENG** 1 hr; **COST** $25; **INIT** N; **ACMP** Y; **NEWS** Y; **PERF** Private recitals; **EDEX** B.M., Augustana College; B.S., Juilliard. Private study with Mario Berini & Felix Knight. Robert Shaw Chorale; Hartt Opera; soloist, New York Choral Society, Amor Artis Chorale; 25 years accompanist & partner with Lucy Lowe in her Song Show.

COMM Specialties: baroque music & German lieder. Good results all ages; main work, college-age students.

NAME   EMMONS, SHIRLEE***
ADDR   12 West 96th Street, New York, NY 10025   212/222-5154
PFFL NATS, NYSTA, League of Women Composers, American Music Center, CMS; **DAYS** Wed.–Fri., including evenings; **AFFL** Boston University, AIMS Summer Vocal Institute in Graz, Tanglewood Institute; **LENG** 1 hr; **COST** $50; **INIT** $30; **ACMP** N; **NEWS** Y; **PERF** Small workshops & private recitals; **EDEX** Lawrence University, Appleton, WI; Curtis Institute; Conservatorio Giuseppe Verdi, Milan. Recordings on RCA Victor, Concert Hall. NBC Opera, American Opera Company, Santa Fe Opera, Columbia concert tours.

COMM Co-author of book *The Art of the Song Recital* (Schirmer).

NAME   ESPINA, DR. NONI
ADDR   220 W. 98th Street, Apt. 9-J, New York, NY 10025   212/866-5188
PFFL NATS, NYSTA, ASCAP; **DAYS** 7, including evenings; **AFFL** City University of New York; **LENG** 1 hr; **COST** $25+; **INIT** $5; **ACMP** N; **NEWS** Y; **PERF** N; **FAME** Many; **EDEX** Two master's degrees in Voice & Ph.D. from Indiana University; Juilliard, School of Sacred Music. Studied with Corleen Weels, Mme. Manski & Sergius Kagen. Numerous recitals throughout world. Twenty years' teaching.

COMM Author of standard references: *Repertoire for the Solo Voice; Music for the Voice* (Kagen), edit. 2nd ed.; *Vocal Solos for Protestant Services.* Coaches English, Italian, German, French, Spanish, Latin & oriental languages.

NAME FAULL, ELLEN
ADDR 300 Central Park West, New York, NY 10024   212/362-1420

NAME FERRO, DANIEL E.
ADDR 300 Central Park West, New York, NY 10024   212/724-6476
PFFL NYSTA, NATS, Manual Garcia International Competition; **DAYS** Mon., Wed., Fri.—days only; **AFFL** Voice faculty, Juilliard School; **LENG** 1 hr; **COST** Varies; **INIT** Varies; **ACMP** N; **NEWS** Few; **PERF** Opportunities for recitals in my home; **FAME** Battle, Crespin, Lear, Lindholm, Welting, Ellis, Devlin, Raimondi, Stewart, Stilwell, Titus, Shicoff; **EDEX** B.S., Juilliard; J.A., Columbia; Fulbright, Accademia di Sta. Cecilia, Rome; Accademia Chigiana, Siena; Mozarteum, Salzburg.
COMM Recitals, opera, oratorio & musical theater. Master classes, U.S., Canada, Israel, France, China, Scandinavia, Ireland, England, Adjudicator, Metropolitan Opera Auditions.

NAME FITZ-GERALD, ROBERT
ADDR 160 W. 71st Street, Apt. 3-K, New York, NY 10023   212/877-5445
PFFL AGVA, AFTRA, NYSTA, NATS; **TLOC** N.J. (and NYC); **DAYS** Mon.–Sat., including evenings; **LENG** 1 hr; **COST** $40; **INIT** Y; **ACMP** N; **NEWS** Y; **PERF** Help qualified students find jobs & performances; **EDEX** Over 400 concert performances throughout U.S. & Europe; extensive performance background.

NAME FOX, SALLY
ADDR 8 E. 83rd Street, New York, NY 10028   212/744-1434
PFFL NYSTA; **DAYS** Tues.–Fri., days only; **LENG** 1 hr; **COST** $30–35; **INIT** N; **ACMP** N; **NEWS** Y; **EDEX** Languages at Hunter, theory with Dr. George Powlers (FMD), voice with Sergius Kagen & Ruth Diehl. Eighteen years at Temple Emanu-El; soloist at St. Mark's Church in the Bowery & Christ Methodist Church, New York City.
COMM Specialize in sacred music & lieder.

NAME GARDELLA, KATHERINE J.
ADDR 2109 Broadway, New York, NY 10023   212/877-6494
EDEX Pupil of Genario Mario Curci, brother-in-law & artistic advisor of Amelita Galli-Curci.
COMM No set rules.

NAME GARRISI, PETRA
ADDR 100-17 Einstein Loop, New York, NY 10475   212/379-4324
PFFL NYSTA; **TLOC** Carnegie Hall; **DAYS** Mon. – Wed., Sat., including evenings; **LENG** 1 hr; **COST** $35; **INIT** N; **ACMP** Y; **NEWS** Y; **PERF** Private recitals; **FAME** Ernestine Jackson (*Guys and Dolls* on Broadway); **EDEX** Pupil of Goeta Lyungberg & Ruth Dawson. Michigan Opera Company, Detroit Opera Guild, American Guild of Musical Artists Opera Company. Soloist Town Hall, Carnegie Hall, Park Avenue Methodist Church.

NAME GERARDI, BOB
ADDR 160 W. 73rd Street, New York, NY 10023   212/874-6436
PFFL AFTRA, SAG, AEA, NYSTA, NATS, ASCAP, AGAC, NSAI, NARAS, AFM Local 802; **DAYS** Mon. – Sat., including evenings; **LENG** 45 min; **COST** $25; **INIT** N; **ACMP** N; **NEWS** Y; **PERF** Showcases, club dates, auditions; **EDEX** Studied voice with Richard Field; studied piano, dance, acting, composition. Experience as nightclub singer, pianist, bandleader at hotels, resorts.
COMM Author, *Opportunities in Music* (National Textbook Company).

NAME GRAF, UTA
ADDR 315 W. 86th Street, Apt. 6-A, New York, NY 10024   212/496-1299
DAYS Mon. – Fri.; **AFFL** Manhattan School of Music; **LENG** 55 min; **INIT** $25; **ACMP** Y; **NEWS** Y; **PERF** Master classes, lied course at Manhattan School, seminars; **EDEX** Performed opera, oratorio, recitals, operetta & chamber music under Karajan, Kubelik, Fritz Busch, Kleiber, Leinsdorf, Ormandy, Serafin, Solti, Stokowski; Juilliard Quartet. Opera at San Francisco, Netherlands, Covent Garden, Duesseldorf, Cologne, Aachen, Dresden, Munchen.
COMM Faculty, New England Conservatory & Aspen.

NAME HALLER, GRETCHEN
ADDR 309 N. Washington Street, Herkimer, NY 13350   315/866-3576
PFFL NATS, NYSTA, Sigma Alpha Iota; **TLOC** New York State for 6 months/yr; **DAYS** 7 days, evenings & weekends; **LENG** 45 min; **COST** $25; **INIT** Y; **ACMP** Self; **NEWS** Y; **PERF** Yes; **EDEX** B.M., Roosevelt Musical College—Chicago; Juilliard, studies at Cornell, studies in Milano, Austria, London.
COMM Have sung at opera houses in major cities of U. S.

NAME HAUSER, EMMY
ADDR 730 Riverside Drive, New York, NY 10031   212/368-7534

PFFL NYSTA, NATS; **DAYS** Mon.–Fri., evenings & weekends; **LENG** 1 hr+; **COST** $35; **INIT** N **ACMP** Y; **NEWS** Y; **PERF** Several; **EDEX** European

COMM Held several seminars on vocal technique at Federal City College of the University of the District of Columbia. Function often as judge at major competitions.

NAME HEILWEIL, MAGGI
ADDR 539 E. 78th Street, New York, NY 10021   212/734-6889

PFFL NATS; **DAYS** Varies; evenings & weekends; **LENG** 45 to 60 min; **INIT** Y; **ACMP** Self; **NEWS** Y; **PERF** Private recitals; **EDEX** B.M., Hartt College—Hartford; graduate study at Guildhall School of Music & Drama—London. Have done recitals & opera work here & in London.

COMM Work in individualized way. Have strong working knowledge of physiology of singing along with creative approach to getting students to reach vocal, musical, dramatic potential. Holistic approach involves bio-energetics & consideration of psychological blocks.

NAME HOFFMANN, CYNTHIA
ADDR 316 W. 84th Street, #3-F, New York, NY 10024   212/874-3754

PFFL AGMA, AFTRA, NATS, NYSTA; **AFFL** Faculty, Manhattan School of Music; **COST** TBA; **INIT** Y; **ACMP** Y

NAME HOSWELL (VAN DER MARK), MARGARET***
ADDR 320 West End Avenue, New York, NY 10023   212/787-3037

AFFL Faculty, Manhattan School of Music

COMM Former faculty member of AIMS Summer Vocal Institute in Graz, Austria.

NAME HOUSER, THOMAS H.
ADDR 309 E. Main Street, New Holland, PA 17557   717/354-2228

PFFL NATS, NYSTA, IARS; **TLOC** PA and 2109 Broadway, #977 212/874-1279; **DAYS** Fri., Sat., evenings & weekends; **LENG** ½ or 1 hr; **COST** $50/hr; **INIT** Y; **ACMP** Self; **NEWS** Y; **EDEX** Certif/voice, Peabody Conservatory; B.A., Goddard College; M.A., Norwich Univ. Studied voice with Elizabeth Valdes, Tito Schipa, Gilda della Rizza, Oren Brown; movement & awareness with Elaine Summers, Moshe Feldenkrais.

COMM Innovator of Explorations in Singing—unique series of workshops & master classes integrating vocal technique, repertoire, body awareness, movement. Specialty: technique & its application to literature.

NAME JOHNSON, BEVERLEY
ADDR 257 W. 86th Street, New York, NY 10024
AFFL Faculty, Juilliard; adjunct faculty, Brooklyn College, CUNY

NAME JONES, DAVID L.
ADDR 166 W. 94th Street, #4-B, New York, NY 10025   212/749-4364
PFFL NATS, founder of NY Voice Workshop series & Amsterdam Voice Workshop; **DAYS** Mon. – Sat., weekends; **AFFL** New York Voice Workshop Series; **LENG** 1 hr; **COST** $30; **INIT** N; **NEWS** Y; **PERF** Small workshops, ensemble recitals, workshops for voice instructor; **FAME** Karen Grahn; **EDEX** Texas Christian University, North Texas State University, special studies in speech therapy. Juilliard Voice Foundation. Soloist—New York Community Choral Organization.
COMM Instructor by invitation—Akademie Voor Kleinkunst, Amsterdam, Holland.

NAME JOSEPH, EMMY
ADDR 411 West End Avenue, New York, NY 10024   212/873-0006
PFFL Dalcroze School of Music, NYSTA; **DAYS** Mon. – Sat., days only; **LENG** 1 hr; **COST** $40; **INIT** N; **ACMP** You provide; **NEWS** Y; **PERF** Private recitals; **FAME** Larry Kert, Ken Marshall, Brent Barrett, Marcy de Gonge; **EDEX** Ph.D. University of Heidelberg. Opera and concert appearances in Europe.

NAME KERR, JAY
ADDR 1595 Broadway, #413, New York, NY 10019   212/582-5118
PFFL AFM, NCEA, ASCAP; Manhattan Theatre Workshop; **DAYS** Mon. – Fri., evenings; **AFFL** California State University—Northridge; **LENG** 55 min; **COST** $30; **INIT** N; **ACMP** Provided; **NEWS** Y; **PERF** Small workshops; those qualified sing at a top NY cabaret; **FAME** Bob Gunton, Jane Oliver, Ina Balin, Hugh Brannum, Barry Manilow; **EDEX** Performed on & written for Broadway. M.A., Cal State University. Studied with Milt Lyon, Stephan Porter, Kenneth McMillan. Producer &/or director of Musical Theatre in Hollywood & New York.
COMM Singing for Broadway is melodic extension of speaking voice. Everyone can produce full natural sound. We find, define, improve upon it. Specialties: singing for musical theatre, auditioning for musicals.

NAME KOGUT, LORETTA I.
ADDR 434 E. 58th Street, New York 10022   212/755-8349
PFFL NATS, NYSTA, NOA, AGMA, AAUW; Board, Community Opera of New

York; **DAYS** Mon., Wed., Thurs.; **LENG** 45 min; **COST** $20; **INIT** $10; **ACMP** You provide; **NEWS** Y; **PERF** Private recitals; **EDEX** M.S. in Voice, Juilliard School. Opera & concert performances—solo & ensemble.

NAME LAVANNE, ANTONIA
ADDR 210 W. 101st Street, New York, NY 10025   212/866-1190
PFFL NATS, NYSTA, MTNA, The Bohemians; **DAYS** Every day but Thurs.; **AFFL** Mannes College of Music, Roundtop Festival, California Music Center; **LENG** 1 hr; **INIT** $30; **ACMP** Provided; **NEWS** N; **PERF** Small workshops, private recitals; **FAME** Seth McCoy, Karen Johnson, Barbara Martin; **EDEX** Budapest Academy (violin); Rubin Academy, Jerusalem (voice). Study with Jennie Tourel & Lotte Leonard. Aspen, Tanglewood. Recitals, chamber music, orchestra soloist, opera.
COMM Complete training in technique & musical preparation. Languages coached: German, French, Italian, Hungarian, Hebrew.

NAME LEARY, MARGARET
ADDR 46 Grandview Avenue, Glen Rock, NJ 07452   201/444-2382
PFFL AEA, SAG, AFTRA, NATS, SAI; **TLOC** New Jersey; **DAYS** Mon.–Sat./ evenings & Sat. a.m.; **LENG** 1 hr; **COST** $25; **INIT** N; **ACMP** Y; **NEWS** Y; **PERF** Small workshops, private recitals; **EDEX** American Conservatory & New York. Opera performances in Chicago, New York, Philadelphia & London. Concert & recital work in U. S. & England; in stock, regional & dinner theaters, TV.
COMM Specialize in training of serious vocal artist in all fields at performance level.

NAME LEVY, NED
ADDR 115 E. 9th Street, #3-A, New York, NY 10003   212/674-5474
PFFL NATS, AEA, SAG, AFM Local 802; **DAYS** Tues.–Sat.; **AFFL** Former assistant professor, University of Illinois; **LENG** 1 hr; **ACMP** Self; **NEWS** Y; **PERF** Small workshops; **FAME** Anny De Gange, Darla Hill, Susan Edwards; **EDEX** B.A., Millikin University; M.A., Ph.D., University of Illinois. Opera, oratorio, musical comedy, drama. Musical direction, La Mama, WPA Theater, Circle Repertory, *Torch Song Trilogy.*
COMM Coaching provided only for own students; classical repertoire & pop.

NAME LIGHTNER, DR. HELEN L.
ADDR 175 W. 76th Street, #12-C, New York, NY 10023   212/787-7626

PFFL NYSTA, NATS, AAUP, MENC; **DAYS** Weekends; **AFFL** New York University; **LENG** 1 hr; **INIT** Y; **ACMP** N; **NEWS** Y; **PERF** Small workshops, private recitals; **EDEX** B.M., M.M., Ed.D. Various major cities in U. S. & abroad.

NAME LIKOVA, EVA
ADDR 2109 Broadway, #17–104, New York, NY 10023   212/595-0075

DAYS 7 days, evenings; **AFFL** Professor emeritus, University of Michigan; **LENG** 30, 45, 60 min; **COST** $30, $42.50, $50; **INIT** $25; **ACMP** N; **NEWS** Few; **PERF** Small workshops, private recitals; **FAME** Sarah Arneson, Julia Conwell, Marybeth Smith, Susan Anthony, Carlos Chausson, Gordon Finlay; Thomas Pederson; Melanie Kimball; **EDEX** Performed with N.Y.C. Opera & many international houses. Taught, directed, performed for 16 years at University of Michigan.

COMM Continuing in NYC a practice begun in Michigan, is presenting annually "Opera Gems in Solo and Ensemble," opportunity for students to perform scenes. Specializes in bel canto principles, easy high notes & coloratura, mixed head-chest resonances for easy, strong forte.

NAME LLOYD, WHITFIELD
ADDR RFD #2, Katonah, NY 10536   212/724-7150

PFFL NATS, AGMA; **TLOC** 170 W. 73rd Street, #5-C, New York City; **DAYS** Mon., Tues., Thurs.—days; **AFFL** 25 yrs. professor of voice & opera at Marymount College; **LENG** 55 min; **COST** $45; **INIT** $45; **ACMP** Provided; **NEWS** Y; **FAME** Scott Reene, Phyllis Hunter, Julia Lovett, Barbara Hocher; **EDEX** B.M., Manhattan School of Music. Performed with various opera companies; soloist with N.Y. Philharmonic. Recitals, oratorio & orchestra engagements.

COMM Because I direct opera in regional companies, I can recommend advanced students to these companies.

NAME LOVETRI, JEANNETTE
ADDR 212 W. 80th Street, #3-W, New York, NY 10024   212/799-0407

PFFL NATS, NYSTA, AGMA; **DAYS** Mon.–Fri., evenings; **AFFL** Former faculty member, Upsala College, N.J.; **LENG** 40 min; **COST** $30/20; **INIT** N; **ACMP** You provide; **NEWS** Y; **FAME** G. Benedict, M. Gorrill, Sp. Ford, T. Homberg, S. Reece, M. Monk; **EDEX** Performed in opera, oratorio, studio, gospel, cabaret, off-Broadway, stock & jazz. Attended Manhattan School of Music & Juilliard. Extensive background in healing arts—meditation, yoga, bodywork.

COMM Specialize in repairing damage & clarifying stylistic vs. technical differences. Am consultant to corporations on vocal problems & director of The Voice Workshop—seminar for executives.

NAME LOZADA, ANGELICA
ADDR 45 Grove Street, #3-C, New York, NY 10014   212/255-9130
PFFL NATS, NYSTA, Bohemians Club; **DAYS** Tues.–Thurs. & weekends; **AFFL** William Paterson State College, N.J.; **LENG** 1 hr; **COST** $35; **INIT** $20 **ACMP** You provide; **NEWS** Y; **EDEX** Graduate of Juilliard & Manhattan School of Music. Recitals in Town Hall, Carnegie Hall. Performed with opera companies in U.S. & Europe; Hansestadt Theater—Luebeck; Muenchener Bach Chor.
COMM Fifteen years' European experience. Fluent in five languages. Teachers: Florence P. Kimball, John Brownlee, Paula Frijsch, Mme. Huni-Mihacsek, Luigi Ricci, Mme. Maragliano-Mori.

NAME MALAS, MARLENA
ADDR 245 W. 104th Street, New York, NY 10025   212/749-2615

NAME MAREK, DAN
ADDR 210 W. 101st Street, #10-F, New York, NY 10025   212/222-1546
PFFL NATS, College Music Society, AGMA; **DAYS** Tues.–Sat.; **AFFL** Mannes College of Music; **LENG** ½ or 1 hr; **COST** $40/hr; **INIT** N; **ACMP** Y; **NEWS** Y; **PERF** Small workshops, private recitals; recommendations for professionals; **FAME** Robert Mandan, Ruth Kobart, Joachim Romaguera, Charles Abruzzo; **EDEX** B.M., M.M., Manhattan School of Music. Vocal study—John Brownlee, Jerome Hines. Principal tenor: Metropolitan Opera, Salzburg Opera, N.Y.C. Opera. Orchestral appearances with Leopold Stokowski, Eduardo Mata.
COMM Much of my teaching is based on teachings of bel canto masters combined with modern research.

NAME Mc LAUGHLIN, GENE
ADDR 2109 Broadway, #13-41, New York, NY 10023   212/787-4982
PFFL NATS, NYSTA; **DAYS** Tues.–Sat.; **LENG** ½ or 1 hr; **INIT** N; **NEWS** Y; **PERF** Small workshops & private recitals; **EDEX** Conservatorio G. Verdi-Milano; private studies with Campo Galliani, G. Consiglio, Oren Brown, Maude Tweedy. Opera performances throughout Western Europe.
COMM Specialties—Broadway (classical bel canto approach).

NAME MICHALSKI, NADINE
ADDR 125 Lincoln Avenue, Elizabeth, NJ 07208   212/351-9746
PFFL NATS, Actors Equity; **DAYS** Mon.–Sat.; **LENG** 45 min; **COST** $20; **INIT** $20; **ACMP** Y; **NEWS** Y; **EDEX** B.M., Lawrence University; M.A., Colum-

bia. Soprano soloist in opera & oratorio; NBC Opera; musical director in summer stock; accompanist in over 90 recitals in U.S. & Canada.

COMM Easily reached by train from Penn Station in 20 minutes.

NAME MINTER, DREW
ADDR 292 W. 92nd Street, #5-C, New York, NY 10025   212/787-5167
PFFL Concert Royal, Pomerium Musices; **DAYS** Wed.–Sat., days; **AFFL** Wagner College; **LENG** 1 hr; **COST** $25; **INIT** $25; **ACMP** N; **NEWS** Y; **EDEX** B.S., Indiana University; diploma, Vienna Hochschule fur Musik. Studies with Marcy Lindheimer, Carl Stough. Professional performances in opera & concert in U.S. & Europe.

COMM Specialize in breathing coordination, based on Stough Method, Alexander Technique & Feldenkrais Method.

NAME MOK, ELLIE MAO
ADDR 14 Colonial Avenue, Larchmont, NY 10538   914/834-1360
PFFL NYSTA, AMTL, MELO; WMTG; **TLOC** 2109 Broadway, New York City; **DAYS** Mon., Wed., Fri.; evenings; **AFFL** Hoff-Bartholson Music School— SUNY Purchase; **LENG** 1 hr; **COST** $35; **INIT** $15; **ACMP** $10; **NEWS** Y; **PERF** Small workshops, private recitals; operatic performance for qualified; **EDEX** Juilliard School, Columbia University, Vienna. Recitals in Town Hall, Carnegie Hall, major cities of world. Soloist with Vienna Bach Society, Honolulu Symphony, Peking Philharmonic Society.

COMM Method is scientific approach to bel canto singing. Principles of William Vennard's method applied. Special attention to diction, style & interpretation of songs.

NAME MONBO, HELENA W.
ADDR 160 W. 73rd Street, #3-C, New York, NY 10023   212/877-4168
PFFL NATS; **DAYS** Mon.–Fri.; evenings; **LENG** ½ or 1 hr; **COST** $50/hr; **INIT** Y; **ACMP** Y; **NEWS** Y; **FAME** Robert Edwin, Roy Allan Wilson, Deborah Geffner, Grace Jones; **EDEX** Over 50 years' experience as voice & speech teacher & therapist. Mannes College of Music, Essex County Overbrook Hospital.

COMM Voice & speech dynamics in total personality is holistic, scientific & intensely personal pedagogical method. Human voice is part of whole person—a flesh & blood instrument that cannot be separated from thoughts, feelings & physical health.

NAME MOORE, DOROTHY RUDD
ADDR 33 Riverside Drive, New York, NY 10023   212/787-1869
PFFL NYSTA, BMI, American Composers Alliance, American Women Composers; **DAYS** Mon.–Fri.; evenings; **LENG** 1 hr; **COST** $25; **INIT** N; **ACMP** You provide; **NEWS** Y; **EDEX** Am composer–singer. B.M., Howard University. Studied in France. Voice at Howard University & in New York.

COMM Teach voice, sightsinging, ear-training & piano. Happily accept beginning students. In all cases stress that my students become musicians. Sightsinging is taught separately from voice lesson.

NAME NASSIF, ROBERT LINDSEY
ADDR 375 South End Avenue, #2-J, New York, NY 10280 212/912-0819
PFFL NYSTA, Pi Kappa Lambda Music Honors Society, BMI; **TLOC** Carnegie Hall, 881 Seventh Avenue; **LENG** 1 hr; **COST** $32; **INIT** N; **NEWS** Y; **EDEX** BGS and Master of Fine Arts in Voice–University of Iowa. Sommerakademie, Mozarteum, Salzburg.

COMM Am specialist in diagnosis of muscle misuse & vocal rebuilding. Teachings are original & based on latest scientific research. Laws of physics & acoustics are integrated in technique which develops, relaxes, involves specific muscle groups.

NAME NAUM, YVONNE, PH.D.
ADDR 2109 Broadway, #15-60, New York, NY 10023   212/362-4698
DAYS Mon.–Sat., days & evenings; **LENG** 45/60 min; **COST** $30/hr; **INIT** N; **ACMP** Y; **NEWS** Y; **PERF** Small workshops, recitals; **EDEX** B.A., Hunter College; Ph.D., Columbia University. Actors' Institute, Oglebay Institute, University of Washington, Verdi Square Opera. Coaches five languages.

COMM A lyric-spinto soprano, I specialize in roles of Aida, Tosca, Turandot, Manon Lescaut, Leonora (*Trovatore* & *Forza*), Sieglinde & Elisabeth. Also studied & performed mezzo-soprano roles. Have considerable background in nonoperatic repertoire.

NAME NEWTON, NORMA***
ADDR 7619 Streamside Drive, Houston, TX 77088   713/445-4911
PFFL NATS, Central Opera Service; **TLOC** Home and Bronxville, NY 914/ 337-3734; **DAYS** Thurs.–Mon. (see below); **AFFL** Houston Opera Studio; **LENG** 1 hr; **COST** $55; **INIT** Y; **ACMP** N; **NEWS** Y; **PERF** Workshops & recitals; **FAME** Susanne Mentzer, Carroll Freeman, Robert Galbraith, Kay Pascal; **EDEX** Leading soprano, New York City Opera, Welsh National Opera. European career, 1965–74.

COMM Teach in NYC every fifth week, Thursday–Monday. To reach, phone Bronxville or write or call Houston.

NAME OAS, JUDITH
ADDR 44 W. 62nd Street, #3-C, New York, NY 10023   212/582-9380

NAME OWEN, CHLOE***
ADDR 41 W. 86th Street, New York, NY 10024   212/595-7530
AFFL Boston University; **EDEX** Opera, concert, radio, oratorio, recordings throughout America & Europe, including Salzburg, Spoleto, Munich, Milan, Duesseldorf.
COMM Former faculty member of AIMS Summer Vocal Institute in Graz, Austria.

NAME PICKER, NELLY
ADDR 46 Exton Avenue, North Arlington, NJ 07032   201/991-9080
PFFL NATS, MENC, NEA, NJEA; **TLOC** NJ 201/991-9083; **DAYS** Mon., Wed., Fri., Sat. eve & weekends; **AFFL** Music Studio for the Performer, 232 Belleville Tnpk, N. Arlington; **LENG** 30/45 min; **COST** $20; **INIT** N; **NEWS** Y; **PERF** Small workshops, private recitals, showcases; **EDEX** Vienna States Academy, Conservatorio di G. Verdi—Milano. Radio, opera, concerts in Europe & Middle East.
COMM Specialty: bel canto for coloratura & lyric sopranos.

NAME PORRELLO, JOSEPH
ADDR 53 W. 11th Street, New York, NY 10011   212/989-1306
PFFL AGMA, AFTRA, Equity, SAG, NYSTA; **TLOC** Service: 212/724-7400; **DAYS** Mon.–Sat.; **LENG** 1hr; **COST** $35; **INIT** Y; **ACMP** N; **NEWS** Y; **PERF** Access to professionals in NYC; **EDEX** B.M., M.M., Manhattan School; special studies at Juilliard. Performances with Metropolitan, San Francisco & Santa Fe operas, National Symphony, Opera Orchestra of NY, Newport Festival, Amalfi Festival (Italy).
COMM Have performed in musical comedy & light opera & am comfortable teaching students in these styles.

NAME RADEBAUGH, DAN
ADDR 36 Plaza Street, #2-G, Brooklyn, NY 11238   212/442-5324
PFFL NATS; **TLOC** 129 West 67th Street, New York, NY 10023; **DAYS** Mon.–

Sat.; evenings & weekends; **LENG** ½ or 1 hr; **COST** $30; **INIT** N; **ACMP** N; **NEWS** Y; **PERF** Private recitals; **EDEX** B.A. & M.M., University of South Florida. Adjunct faculty—University of South Florida. Voice faculty—Armstrong State College. Performed in opera, oratorio, musicals, theater & recitals.

NAME RASKIN, JUDITH
ADDR 535 E. 86th Street, New York, NY 10028   212/988-1083

PFFL AGMA, AFTRA, NATS; **DAYS** Varies; **AFFL** Manhattan School of Music, Mannes, 92nd St. Y; **LENG** Varies; **COST** $60/hr; **INIT** Y; **ACMP** Y; **NEWS** N; **PERF** Performances at 92 St. Y, through the Master Classes for Opera Singers; **EDEX** B.A., M.A. (Hon.)—Smith College, D.M. (Hon.)—Ithaca College. Metropolitan, New York City, and Santa Fe operas. Glyndebourne Festival Opera. Soloist with major orchestras.

COMM Conduct many master classes & specialize in repertoire ranging from pre-18th century to present-day music. Teaching time is limited. Seek only artist-calibre students.

NAME READING, CHARLES G.
ADDR 257 W. 86th Street, New York, NY 10024   212/877-7573

PFFL NATS, NYSTA; **DAYS** 7 days; **LENG** 1 hr; **COST** $50; **ACMP** Y; **NEWS** Y; **FAME** In 35 years of teaching, has prepared many students for successful auditions. Associated with Giuseppe De Luca & authorized to carry on his work; **EDEX** Educated in piano and languages, including at Juilliard.

COMM Specialty: bel canto school.

NAME REED, V. WILLIAM
ADDR 890 West End Avenue, Apt. 1-A, New York, NY 10023 212/724-3134

PFFL NATS, NYSTA, AGMA, IAERS; **TLOC** 200 W. 70th St., Apt. 15-K; 865-4404; **DAYS** Mon.–Sat.; **LENG** 30, 45, 60 min; **COST** $45; **INIT** Y; **ACMP** Y; **NEWS** Y; **PERF** Studio, chamber opera company, summer voice seminar—Marywood College; **EDEX** Ed.D., Teachers College, Columbia University. Extensive performing career, especially in concerts & oratorio; eight years' university teaching.

NAME REPP, ELLEN
ADDR 50 W. 67th Street, New York, NY 10023   212/595-0184

NAME REXDALE, THOMAS A.
ADDR 2109 Broadway, New York, NY 10023   212/870-1418

PFFL AGMA, NYSTA, Bohemians; **DAYS** Mon.–Sat., evenings & weekends; **LENG** 1 hr; **COST** $35; **INIT** $35; **ACMP** Y; **NEWS** Y; **PERF** Small workshops, private recitals; **FAME** Margaret Taylor—female vocalist for Glenn Miller, Fandango; **EDEX** M.A., Vocal Pedagogy, Teachers College, Columbia Univ.; B.M.E., Augustana College, Rock Island, Ill. Soloist with N.Y. Philharmonic, Musica Sacra, N.Y. Mendelssohn Club. Central City Opera Co., recordings, radio, and TV.

COMM Extensively studied teaching of Polish tenor & teacher, Jean de Reszke, & worked directly with many of his students. Work on vocal technique from opera to rock, from beginners to seasoned professionals.

NAME   ROBERTSON, SCOTT
ADDR   484 W. 43rd Street, #32-L, New York, NY 10036   212/244-2649
PFFL Actors Equity, AFTRA, Screen Actors Guild; **DAYS** Mon.–Sat., evenings & weekends; **AFFL** Drake University; **LENG** 1 hr; **COST** $20; **INIT** N; **ACMP** Y; **NEWS** Y; **FAME** Treat Williams & other Broadway & film actors for musicals & cabaret; **EDEX** Have appeared on Broadway, off-Broadway, TV & films in principal musical roles, including *Grease, Scrambled Feet* & *Applause.* Sing jingles & national TV commercials—Dr. Pepper, etc.

COMM Studied with Ryan Edwards; extensive workshops in vocal coaching for theater auditions.

NAME   RODGERS, LOU
ADDR   144 W. 11th Street, New York, NY 10011   212/691-6105
PFFL Actors Equity, AGMA, ART, BMI, Artistic Director—Golden Fleece, Ltd.; **DAYS** Mon.–Fri., some evenings; **AFFL** St. Johns University, Brooklyn Technical College; **LENG** 1 hr; **COST** $25; **INIT** N; **ACMP** N; **NEWS** Y; **PERF** Some; **EDEX** NY City Opera, Santa Fe Opera, Broadway, regional theater, summer stock, off-Broadway.

COMM Specialize in bel canto. For musical theater, train dancers & actors to sing basic vocal technique.

NAME   ROGERS, EARL
ADDR   920 Riverside Drive, New York, NY 10032   212/799-9831
PFFL AFTRA, SAG, NATS, NYSTA, Academy of Teachers of Singing; **TLOC** Beacon Hotel, Broadway & W. 75th St.; **DAYS** Mon.–Sat., days only; **LENG** 45 min; **COST** $25; **INIT** N; **ACMP** Y; **NEWS** Y; **FAME** Marion Moore, winner of several competitions, including Maria Callas; **EDEX** B.S., Western Reserve University; M.M., Cleveland Institute of Music. Much experience in recitals, church & synagogue, & in training vocal groups for radio & television.

COMM Former faculty Cleveland Institute of Music, Queens College.

NAME ROSS, HEATHER
ADDR 210 Rider Avenue, Malverne, NY 11565   516/599-4053
PFFL NATS; **DAYS** Sat.–Thurs., evenings & weekends; **AFFL** Molloy College; **LENG** 1 hr; **COST** $20; **INIT** N; **ACMP** N; **NEWS** Y; **PERF** Set up auditions for agents & management when student is ready; **EDEX** B.M.–Curtis Institute; M.M.–Indiana University. Performing experience in opera, Staedtische Buehnen, Flensburg, Germany, Schleswig-Holstein Landesbuehne, Germany, on East Coast & in Midwest.
COMM Malverne can be easily reached in approximately 40 minutes from Manhattan by Long Island RR.

NAME RULLMAN, J. FRANCESCA C.
ADDR 19 Cranberry Street, Brooklyn Heights, NY 1120100   212/858-0296
PFFL NATS, NYSTA, Voice Foundation; **DAYS** Mon.–Wed. & some evenings; **AFFL** New England Conservatory of Music; **LENG** 1 hr; **COST** $40; **INIT** N; **ACMP** Y; **NEWS** Y; **EDEX** New England Conservatory of Music. Studies with Maria Kurenko, Maestra Maria Cascioli, Luigi Ricci. Recitals with Giorgio Favaretta, Maggio Musicale Fiorentina.
COMM Teach on limited basis only after retiring from active performing as result of serious illness. Am selective about students but give time generously if student demonstrates potential. Have extensive knowledge of vocal & symphonic repertoire.

NAME SALON, CORINE
ADDR 1064 Brierwood Boulevard, Schenectady, NY 12308 212/861-5570
PFFL NATS, AEA, AGVA, AGMA; **TLOC** 315 E. 73rd St. 518/346-9060; **DAYS** Wed. & Sat., evenings & weekends; **AFFL** Union College; **LENG** 30/60 min; **COST** $25/hr; **INIT** $15; **ACMP** Y; **NEWS** Y; **PERF** Small workshops, private recitals; **EDEX** B.F.A., M.F.A. in Voice—Carnegie Mellon. Eight years' teaching experience. Pittsburgh Opera, Baarga Opera (Italy), Pittsburgh Civic Light Opera, Capital Artists Opera, Repertory Opera Studio, Bel Canto Opera (NYC).
COMM Performance experience & teaching techniques cover many different styles from pop music to opera. Teach not just classical singing but rather healthy vocal technique that can be applied to other styles as well.

NAME SCHEY, MARGIT
ADDR 404 E. 55th Street, New York, NY 10022   212/755-3462
PFFL NATS, NYSTA; **DAYS** Evenings & weekends; **AFFL** 92nd St. Y Music School; **LENG** 45/60 min; **COST** $35/hr; **INIT** N; **ACMP** N; **NEWS** Y; **PERF** Small workshops, private recitals, solo & duet recitals; **FAME** Jeanette Scov-

otti, Catherine Malfitano; **EDEX** Graduate of State Academy in Vienna, Austria; member of Volksoper in Vienna.

COMM Specialize in bel canto; opera and recital; many languages.

NAME SEGAL, JEANNE
ADDR   415 E. 85th Street, #12-E, New York, NY 10028   212/362-8060
PFFL NATS, College Music Society; **DAYS** Mon.–Fri., evenings; **LENG** 1 hr; **COST** $25; **INIT** $25; **ACMP** Y; **PERF** Private recitals; **EDEX** B.M., M.M.— Cleveland Institute of Music. Performed throughout Midwest. Performed with Aspen Music Festival, Opera Barga, Temple Institute Summer Festival; leading roles with Cleveland Opera & Cleveland Opera Theatre.

COMM Former faculty member at Cleveland Institute, Furman University, Converse College.

NAME SHIRLEY, GEORGE***
ADDR   New School for the Arts, 176 N. Fullerton Avenue,
          Montclair, NJ 07042   201/745-4596
PFFL AGMA, AFTRA, NATS, ACTRA, Canadian Actors' Equity, British Equity; **DAYS** Fri.–Sat.; **AFFL** University of Maryland, New School for the Arts (Montclair); **LENG** 1 hr; **COST** $40; **INIT** Y; **ACMP** Y; **PERF** Small workshops, private recitals, appearances for agencies in U. S.; **EDEX** Leading tenor Metropolitan, San Francisco, & Chicago Operas, Opera Society of Washington, Michigan Opera Theater, Tulsa Opera, Memphis Opera, Royal Opera (Covent Garden), Netherlands Opera.

COMM Specialize in interpretive techniques & vocal technique. Special career development guidance & scholarships offered to qualified students.

NAME SIRASKY, FREDRIC
ADDR   325 W. 45th Street, New York, NY 10036   212/246-0430
PFFL AEA, AGVA, AFM, NATS; **DAYS** Mon.–Fri.; **AFFL** Ensemble Studio Theatre in New York City; **LENG** 1 hr; **COST** $30; **INIT** N; **ACMP** N; **NEWS** Y; **EDEX** M.F.A., Mason Gross School of the Arts, Rutgers University. Am professional actor/singer specializing in musical theater.

COMM Studied and taught with John Powell, Rutgers University.

NAME SKARIMBAS, CAROL BERGEY
ADDR   161 Ames Avenue, Leonia, NJ 07605   201/461-6480
PFFL NATS, AGMA, Equity, AGVA, AFTRA; **TLOC** Home and 365 West End Ave., 874-6506; **DAYS** Mon., Fri., Sat.; **AFFL** Smith College, Vassar College;

LENG 45/60 min; **COST** $35; **INIT** $25; **ACMP** Self; **NEWS** Y; **PERF** Small workshops, private recitals, church recitals; **EDEX** Graduate of Academy of Vocal Arts, Philadelphia. Studied in Bayreuth, Germany. Extensive work in concert & oratorio, radio & TV.

COMM Have performed with NY City, New Orleans, Santa Fe & Philadelphia Lyric Operas, Garden Opera of Philadelphia & in Bielefeld, Hannover & Duesseldorf, Germany. Coach as well as teach.

NAME SMITH, DILYS JONES
ADDR 651 E. 14th Street, #9-H, New York, NY 10009   212/473-6135
PFFL NYSTA, MENC; **DAYS** Mon.–Sat., evenings & weekends; **AFFL** William Paterson College; **LENG** 45 min; **INIT** N; **ACMP** Y; **NEWS** Y; **PERF** Private recitals; **EDEX** Major Bach Festivals in U.S., Leipzig & West Berlin. Performed with colleges & choral groups in Northwest & Midwest & in all major churches in New York City.

NAME SOBOLEWSKA, INGRID
ADDR 345 W. 88th Street, New York, NY 10024   212/763-3102
PFFL NATS, NYSTA (past pres.), The Bohemians; **DAYS** Tues., Thurs.–Sat.; **AFFL** New York University; **LENG** 1 hr; **INIT** N; **NEWS** Y; **PERF** Private recitals; **EDEX** Graduate of Curtis Institute of Music. Studied with Margarete Matzenauer in NYC. Experience in recital, oratorio & opera in U.S. & abroad. Frequent judge of voice competitions in U.S. & Europe.

NAME SPERBER, HERTA
ADDR 155 W. 68th Street, New York, NY 10023   212/362-6778
PFFL NYSTA, NATS; **DAYS** Mon.–Wed., Fri.; **LENG** 1 hr; **COST** $50; **INIT** $25; **NEWS** Y; **PERF** Small workshops, private recitals, auditions; **FAME** Maria Albanese, David Griffith, Bent Norup; **EDEX** Graduate of Vienna Conservatory; student & associate of Arthur Wolf.

COMM Master classes in German lied, German opera. Italian & French schools; German diction for singers.

NAME STARR, RIMA
ADDR 57 W. 75th Street, #2-D, New York, NY 10023   212/787-4993
PFFL Actors Equity, American Association for Music Therapy; **DAYS** 7 days, evenings & weekends; **LENG** 45 min; **COST** $30; **INIT** $30; **ACMP** N; **NEWS** Y; **EDEX** Studied with Jennie Tourel (scholarship); performed in opera, musical comedy & concert. B.S., New York College of Music; M.A., N.Y.U. & Rubin Academy of Music, Jerusalem. Certified music therapist.

COMM Runs groups, workshops & private sessions/lessons combining skills as voice teacher & music therapist. Music therapy is creative-expressive, nonverbal modality emphasizing client's strengths rather than weaknesses.

NAME STEBER, ELEANOR***
ADDR 2109 Broadway, #8-18, New York, NY 10023   212/362-2938
PFFL AGMA, AFTRA, Equity, NATS, NYSTA; **DAYS** Tues.–Fri., NY; weekends, Long Island; **AFFL** Juilliard, SUNY-Purchase, New England Conservatory, Brooklyn College; **LENG** 1 hr; **COST** Negot.; **INIT** $35; **ACMP** N; **NEWS** Y; **PERF** Recitals, workshops, opera scenes for master classes; **EDEX** Twenty-five years leading soprano of Metropolitan Opera. Performed 56 roles in all major opera houses of world & for all leading orchestras. Major international festivals, radio, TV, musical comedy, recordings.

COMM Specialties include operatic arias, oratorio, German lieder, French art songs & American music, stressing Mozart & bel canto styles of singing as taught by Wm. L. Whitney.

NAME SUGARS, JANEAL
ADDR 225 Central Park West, New York, NY 10024   212/496-9214
PFFL NATS, President of Mu Phi Epsilon NY Alum; **DAYS** 7 days, evenings & weekends; **LENG** 30/60 min; **INIT** Y; **NEWS** Y; **PERF** Private recitals, auditions; **EDEX** Professional studies, Juilliard; M.M. in Voice, University of Texas. Actively perform in opera, recital & oratorio in New York, Texas, California & Virginia.

COMM Sing in a healthy way, & you can sing any style you wish. Coach English, Italian, German.

NAME SUSKIND, JOYCE
ADDR 200 W. 70th Street, #9-M, New York, NY 10023   212/362-0135
PFFL NYSTA, American Assoc. Artist Therapists; **DAYS** Mon.–Sat., evenings; **LENG** 45 min; **COST** $40; **INIT** N; **ACMP** Self; **NEWS** Y; **PERF** Provide references to musical productions; **EDEX** Voice & oboe at Juilliard School. Ten years' piano. Performed as singer at Temple Emanu-El & Central Synagogue, NYC. Extensive work as pianist–singer in supper clubs. Soprano soloist with Composer's Ensemble, specializing in 20th century music.

COMM Specialties include Alexander Technique, neuro-linguistic programming, specialty breathing, posture, relaxation, anxiety.

NAME TAYLOR, BERNARD
ADDR 464 Riverside Drive, #42, New York, NY 10027   212/662-6797

DAYS Mon.–Sat.; **AFFL** Juilliard School of Music; **LENG** ½ hr; **COST** $25; **INIT** N; **ACMP** Y; **NEWS** Y; **PERF** Small workshops, private recitals.

NAME   VOLANTE, GLORIA
ADDR   601 Clove Road, Staten Island, NY 10301   212/727-5207

PFFL NYSTA; **DAYS** Mon.–Fri., evenings; **AFFL** College of Staten Island, Music Inst. of the Jewish Comm.; **LENG** 1 hr; **COST** $35; **INIT** N; **ACMP** Y; **NEWS** Y; **PERF** Private recitals; **EDEX** Studied with Harold C. Luckstone, Marinha Gurewitch, Howard Shaw. Studies at Mannes College of Music, College of S. I., Brooklyn Conservatory. Performing at churches & temples in & around NYC.

COMM Extensive work in oratorio, operatic & concert fields. Teach concert repertoire in five languages. Teach sacred music, including Hebrew. Use a combined method of teaching.

NAME   WALL, CATHY
ADDR   825 West End Avenue, New York, NY 10025   212/662-9764

PFFL NATS, NYSTA; **DAYS** Evenings & weekends; **LENG** 1 hr; **COST** $50; **INIT** N; **ACMP** N; **NEWS** Y; **PERF** Can arrange for debut, performances, or study in Italy; **EDEX** B.S., Columbia University. M.A. & M.Ed., Teachers College, Columbia University. Studied for three years in Italy. Performed in Europe & U.S. Speak & coach five languages & Chinese.

COMM Teach how to understand every part of the body & how it is used to find & produce your own beautiful sound.

NAME   WARREN, MICHAEL
ADDR   2350 Broadway, New York, NY 10023   212/874-2298

DAYS Mon.–Sat.; **LENG** ½ or 1 hr; **COST** $55/hr; **INIT** $40; **NEWS** Y; **PERF** Private recitals; **EDEX** D.M.A., University of Maryland. B.M. & M.A., University of Denver.

NAME   WHEELER, MARGARET J.
ADDR   786 Sleepy Hollow Road, Briarcliff Manor, NY 10510 914/271-4825

PFFL AGMA, Actors Equity, NATS; **TLOC** Bennett Conservatory, Croton-on-Hudson; **DAYS** Varies; **AFFL** Bennett Conservatory; **LENG** ½ or 1 hr; **COST** $25/hr; **INIT** N; **NEWS** Y; **PERF** Private recitals, spring recitals at conservatory; **EDEX** M.A.–Hunter College; B.A.–George Peabody College. Studied with Julia Drobner, Thomas Cultice, Thomas Houser, Willard Young, Aida Artsay. Master classes with Oren Brown of Juilliard. Performed with Philadelphia & Staten Island operas.

COMM If enough students were in NYC to warrant it, would be glad to rent studio in city for teaching.

NAME   WHITE, JR., DR. ROBERT C.
ADDR   600 W. 116th Street, #52-A, New York, NY 10027   212/666-5951
PFFL NATS, NYSTA, MTNA, CMS, AAUP; **DAYS** Varies; evenings & weekends; **AFFL** Assoc. professor, Queens College; **LENG** 1 hr; **COST** TBA; **INIT** N; **NEWS** Y; **PERF** Private recitals, association concerts, etc.

NAME   WILKES, RUTH
ADDR   15 Somerset Drive, South, Great Neck, NY 11020   516/466-0348
PFFL NYSTA; **DAYS** Evenings & weekends; **AFFL** Head of Voice Dept., Great Neck School of Music; **LENG** ½ hr; **COST** $20; **INIT** N; **ACMP** Y; **NEWS** Y; **PERF** Small workshops, private recitals, show cases in various hospitals; **FAME** Pat Cantor Sheridan; **EDEX** New England Conservatory: studied with Possony, Frish, Koundoury. Studied with Fred Steele, Oren Brown. Have given many recitals & concerts on radio. Directed TV series for N.Y. State University. Performed in opera.
COMM Preparing workshops in New York & Los Angeles. Specialize in Alexander Technique—relaxation and breathing.

NAME   WOLPERT, RUTH
ADDR   525 West End Avenue, New York, NY 10024   212/362-4559
PFFL NATS, NYSTA; **DAYS** Evenings & weekends; **AFFL** SUNY-Purchase; **LENG** 1 hr; **COST** $30; **INIT** N; **ACMP** N; **NEWS** Y; **PERF** Private recitals; make recommendations through professional connections; **FAME** David Britton, William Shatner, Diana Toscano; **EDEX** Capital University-Conservatory. B.S. & M.A.—Hunter College. Performed in Europe & U.S.

NAME   WORTHINGTON, FLOYD G.
ADDR   22 Tower Drive, Springfield, NJ 07081   201/467-2675
PFFL General manager—Community Opera of NJ, Inc.; **TLOC** Home and 160 W. 71st St., 877-5445; **DAYS** Mon., Wed., Sat. in NYC; **LENG** 1 hr; **COST** $35; **INIT** Y; **ACMP** Y; **NEWS** Y; **PERF** Private recitals, workshops. In professional opera when qualified; **FAME** Bonnie Murray, Edward Watts, Betty Grimn, Dita Delman; **EDEX** Performed throughout Europe, U.S., Canada, Orient. Have toured with major opera companies, symphony orchestras & many oratorio societies. Have produced & directed many operas.
COMM Direct opera workshops, voice technique & voice building. Believe in common sense training of the voice.

NAME   ZUCKER, STEFAN
ADDR   11 Riverside Drive, New York, NY 10023   212/877-1595

PFFL Assoc. for Furtherment of Bel Canto, AFBC Records, WKCR-FM; **DAYS** 7 days, evenings & weekends; **LENG** 1 hr; **COST** $45; **INIT** $45; **ACMP** Y; **NEWS** Y; **PERF** Radio appearances, recordings, major concert hall performances; **EDEX** Juilliard, Hartt, Mozarteum, New England Conservatory, Columbia Univ. & N.Y.U. Performed at Fisher, Town & Merkin concert halls, in Europe & on radio & TV. Contributor to *Opera News, Am. Record Guide.*

COMM Teach technique most widely used during Rossini – Bellini period. Its exponents have had uncommon agility, breath control & range. With it, extended my top by nearly an octave & am listed in *Guinness* as world's highest tenor.

AIMS Seminar, "The Professional Singer's New York"
c/o American Institute of Musical Studies
2701 Fondren Drive
Dallas, TX 75206
214/691-6451

AIMS offers annual seminars in New York City which introduce the performer to the music business and to specific areas of study.

Jim Coleman
724-2800 ("Faces" Company)

Audition techniques for musical theater performers.

Joan Dornemann***
c/o Judith Finell MusicServices Inc.
155 W. 68th Street
New York, NY 10023
580-4500

Ms. Dornemann, a leading coach and assistant conductor at the Metropolitan Opera, offers regular master classes in auditioning and in interpretation. She is a member of the AIMS Faculty at the Summer Vocal Institute in Graz, Austria.

Jeffrey Zeiner
245-1237, 724-2800 (messages)

Audition and career development for show business.

Tracking down the acting classes available to singers was one important reason for producing this book. The following list includes stage directors who do not work in a regular class, along with classes offered on a regular basis. For many we have listed only a telephone contact because the address is often private and is not the same as the location of the course. Whenever possible, we have included prices and other information. We have marked with three asterisks (***) the individuals whom we at AIMS have worked with and know to be effective.

Code

NAME   Name

ADDR   Full address of teaching location (when available) and telephone

COST   Cost per lesson, session or series of classes

COMM   Comments on type of instruction

NAME   ACTORS ADVENT LTD.   242-3900
COMM Limited to 12 per class, career guidelines

NAME   ACTORS AND DIRECTORS LAB INC.; JACK GARFEIN
ADDR   412 W. 42nd Street, 10036   695-5429
COMM Full-time program. Extensive use of scenes and monologues.

NAME   ACTORS INSTITUTE
ADDR   5 W. 19th Street, 3rd floor, 10011   924-8888
COMM Shakespeare

NAME   ACTORS MOVEMENT STUDIO, INC.
COMM (see listing under "Dance and Body Movement Classes")

NAME   JOSEPH BASCETTA
ADDR   8 W. 75th Street, 10023   724-9723
COMM Mr. Bascetta is an opera stage director who regularly holds acting classes for singers. Highly recommended.

NAME   ELINOR BASESCU ACTING STUDIO
ADDR   529 W. 42nd Street, #8D, 10036   868-1278
COST Ms. Basescu's classes cost $15 for class work and $25 per hour for private instruction.

NAME   BEL CANTO OPERA WORKSHOP
ADDR   Robert F. Wagner Junior High School, 220 E. 76th Street, 10021
                                                                535-5231
COST $325 for eight weeks, including scenes performed in public.
COMM Program for opera singers exclusively. Warm-up technique, musical preparation and interpretation, audition skills, role creation, movement, public scenes performed.

NAME   JANET BOOKSPAN***
ADDR   155 W. 68th Street, #1414, 10023   496-0740
COMM Private classes. Ms. Bookspan is an active opera stage director and drama coach. Role development; character study.

NAME   HENRY BUTLER***
ADDR   56 Irving Place, 10003   473-3257
COMM Mr. Butler is an active opera stage director who has done several productions for the Metropolitan Opera. He is a regular member of the faculty at the AIMS Summer Vocal Institute in Graz, Austria.

NAME   CSC REPERTORY COMPANY (City Stage Company)
ADDR   136 E. 13th Street, 10003   677-4210
COST Varies with classes.
COMM Classic scenes study, Shakespeare, stage combat and voice, taught by CSC founder/artistic director Christopher Martin and members of the professional acting company.

NAME   CIRCLE IN THE SQUARE THEATRE
ADDR   1633 Broadway, 10019   581-3270
COST Professional workshop, $3,475; summer workshop, $750.
COMM Individual attention in small classes. Deals with both the traditional and experimental aspects of professional drama. Prestigious faculty.

NAME DANA COEN
ADDR 400 W. 43rd Street, 10036   594-8680
COMM Private acting coaching and instruction. Mr. Coen has a special interest
in musical acting problems.

NAME THE CORNER LOFT STUDIOS
ADDR 99 University Place (at 12th Street), 10003   228-8728

NAME FRANK CORSARO   541-7600,
                                                    ask for Joseph d'Angerio
COMM Teaches combination opera/acting class on Saturdays.

NAME RICHARD CRITTENDEN   201/836-9122
COMM Mr. Crittenden was for many years an associate of Boris Goldovsky
and is well known for his acting classes.

NAME VICTORIA DEVANY
ADDR 337 W. 14th Street, 10014   764-1711
COST $20
COMM A fun and relaxed environment, where students (ages 15 to 18) can
learn beginning techniques and skills.

NAME MARIE BRIDGET DUNDON
ADDR 43-40 44th Street, Sunnyside, NY 11104   937-9340,
                                            874-5300 (answering service)
COMM Of special interest to actors/singers working on British shows or
audition pieces. Education: Royal Academy of Music.

NAME ROBERT ELSTON
ADDR 112 Charlton Street, 10014   929-4718

NAME ERNIE MARTIN STUDIO THEATRE
ADDR 311 W. 43rd Street, 10036   397-5880,
                                            752-7676 (answering service)
COMM Scenes, improvisation, sensory exercises, character study, script
analysis, private coaching, audition material, vocal coaching, speech, singing,
dance, playwriting, awareness through movement, survival in the theater.

NAME   RICHARD GEDTKE
ADDR   43 W. 73rd Street, 10023   724-1238
COST $85–95 per six-week session
COMM Maximum enrollment ten; also private coaching.

NAME   HAROLD GUSKIN
ADDR   62 Jane Street, 10014   620-0172

NAME   HB STUDIO INC.
ADDR   120 Bank Street, 10014   675-2370
COST $95 for two-hour session, one/week for 19 weeks
COMM Acting, movement, musical comedy, speech, voice. One of the most popular classes in the city.

NAME   JOHN HABER***
ADDR   145 W. 74th Street, 10023   874-0351
COST $30, usually for classes of 8 to 10 weeks
COMM Mr. Haber has been acting coach with the Metropolitan Opera Young Artists Program and is head of the Opera Department at Boston University. Also coaches privately.

NAME   PRUDENCE HOLMES
ADDR   206 W. 88th Street, 10024   595-7273
COST $30
COMM Professor at N.Y.U. and Carnegie Mellon University. Miss Holmes teaches speaking voice and diction.

NAME   RAPHAEL KELLY   840-1234

NAME   LEE STRASBERG THEATRICAL INSTITUTE INC.
ADDR   115 E. 15th Street, 10003   523-5500
COMM Strasberg Method—incorporating some psychodrama, etc. Video tapes; prestigious.

NAME MADELYN J. BURNS SEMINARS INC.
ADDR 1697 Broadway, Room 407, 10019   245-3332
COMM Scene study and other.

NAME PAUL MANN ACTORS WORKSHOP
ADDR 218 W. 47th Street, 10036   877-8575
COMM Professional acting training.

NAME IRENE MOORE   535-7045

NAME SONIA MOORE   755-5120
COMM Stanislavski System; day and evening classes.

NAME MICHAEL MORIARTY   518-0297
COMM Scene study course.

NAME PERFORMERS SEMINAR WORKSHOP
ADDR 243 W. 55th Street, 10019   246-0284
COMM All types and video tapes as well. Intimate studio workshop situation.
Can audit free.

NAME WARREN ROBERTSON THEATRE WORKSHOP***
ADDR 303 E. 44th Street, 10017   687-6430
COST $85–100 for four-week cycle; $40–100 for special classes.
COMM Body movement; speech, dialect, monologue; acting classes; audition
training; musical comedy coaching.

NAME DYLAN ROSS   757-0716
COST $30 for two 3-hour sessions weekly
COMM Mr. Ross is particularly interested in relating styles of acting to bel
canto techniques.

NAME SCHOOL OF THE RIVERSIDE SHAKESPEARE COMPANY OF
          NEW YORK CITY, INC.
ADDR 165 W. 86th Street, 10024   877-6810

COMM Classical pieces—small classes focusing on initial scansion and structural analysis through development as audition material.

NAME   TERRY SCHREIBER ACTING STUDIO
ADDR   31 Washington Square West, 10011   874-7509, 475-9362
COMM Scene exploration of Greek drama, Restoration, Moliere, Shaw, Chekov, Ibsen, Strindberg, Feydeau, Anouilh, Giraudoux and others.

NAME   78th STREET THEATER LAB
ADDR   236 W. 78th Street, 10024   595-0850

NAME   STELLA ADLER CONSERVATORY OF ACTING
ADDR   130 W. 56th Street, 10019   246-1195
COST $300—two terms; 2½-hour session each week for 15 weeks.
COMM Shakespeare

NAME   HARVEY VINCENT   861-3291

NAME   STEPHEN WADSWORTH   982-7255

NAME   JACK WALZER   246-6465, 840-1234
COMM Improvisations, scenes, cold readings.

NAME   WEIST-BARRON SCHOOL OF TELEVISION COMMERCIAL
              ACTING, INC.
ADDR   35 W. 45th Street, 10036   840-7025
COST Cost varies depending upon course study.
COMM Scenes, monologues, improvisations & awareness exercises. Workshop programs limited to 12; highly recommended for commercial work.

NAME   STANLEY ZAREFF
ADDR   119 Montague Street #4, Brooklyn, NY 11201   237-1753
COMM Improvisational acting classes on Wednesday evenings at Tyson Studios, 1026 Avenue of the Americas.

Every singer needs to be in a movement or dance class of some kind. Most of the names listed below are groups which teach multiple dance and/or exercise techniques, not merely classical ballet.

Actors and Directors Lab, Inc.
Jack Garfein, Artistic Director
412 W. 42nd Street
695-5429

Mime and dance

Actors Movement Studio, Inc.
5 W. 31st Street, 6th floor
580-2753

AMS offers classes in basic movement techniques, mime, period-style movement and fencing for the theater. Note: the telephone number is the studio's business office and is not located on W. 31st Street, but it should be used to obtain information.

Floris Alexander
226 W. 56th Street
757-3033

Intermediate, advanced ballet

Alexander Technique American Center
142 West End Avenue (at 66th Street)
799-0468

A large faculty of private instructors who teach the Alexander Technique.

Ballet Arts
#61 Carnegie Hall
154 W. 57th Street
582-3350

Ballet, jazz, modern

Phil Black Dance Studio
1630 Broadway
247-2675

Jazz and tap

Brenda Bufalino
226 W. 56th Street
757-3033

Intermediate tap

Gail Conrad
25 Bleecker Street
673-2048
Tap

The Dance Loft
72 Grove Street
255-2808
Jazz, aerobics, slimnastics

Jerri Garner
124 W. Houston Street
254-3951
Dance for singers and actors only

Peter Gennaro
226 W. 56th Street
757-3033
Intermediate tap

Nanette Glushak
1845 Broadway
582-7929

Hebrew Arts School
129 W. 67th Street
362-8060
Jazz and exercise classes

International Dance School
881 Seventh Avenue (Carnegie Hall)
247-6056
Jazz and ballet

J & J's Stretch Shop
59 E. 11th Street, 6th floor
505-0753, 989-3009
Aerobics, dance

Krause & Company
45 E. 65th Street, 2nd floor
758-2665
Exercise classes, weight training for women

Luigi's Jazz Center
36 W. 62nd Street
247-1995
Said to be popular with Broadway performers.

Billie Mahoney
2291 Broadway (at 82nd Street)
535-6589
Jazz classes, beginning tap

Nat Horne Musical Theatre, Inc.
440 W. 42nd Street, 3rd floor
736-7128
Jazz classes

New Dance Group Studio
254 W. 47th Street
245-9327
Jazz, modern, ballet, tap

New York Conservatory of Dance
Ronnie DeMarco
581-1908

Our Studios
147 W. 24th Street
807-8464
Aerobics, exercise, dance, ballet

Michael Owens
Amity Arts Center
22 W. 15th Street
924-5295
Teacher/choreographer

Joseph Pugliese
36 W. 62nd Street, 3rd floor
Jazz classes

West Side Dance Project
220 W. 80th Street
580-0915
Dance basics for performers

We have marked with three asterisks (***) the teachers whom we at AIMS have worked with and know to be effective. For additional language and diction teachers, see also the list of music schools and conservatories.

Alliance Francaise/French Institute
22 E. 60th Street
New York, NY 10022
355-6100

Raymond Beegle (Russian)***
12 W. 72nd Street
New York, NY 10023
724-5615

Bretta Bracali (Italian)
2109 Broadway
New York, NY 10023
877-7904

Nico Castel (French, German, Italian, Portuguese, Spanish)***
170 West End Avenue, #10-N
New York, NY 10023
799-8014

Mr. Castel is official diction coach for the Metropolitan Opera and a member of the faculty at the AIMS Summer Vocal Institute in Graz, Austria.

Center for Speech Arts (Laura Darius)
200 W. 57th Street, Suite 403
New York, NY 10019
245-1450

Regional and foreign accent correction. Speech and voice training.

Dalcroze School of Music
161 E. 73rd Street
New York, NY 10021
879-0316

Deutsches Haus at New York University
42 Washington Mews
New York, NY 10003
598-2217

Language Lab, Inc.
211 E. 43rd Street
New York, NY 10017
697-2020

Manhattan School of Music
120 Claremont Avenue
New York, NY 10027
749-2802

New School for Social Research
66 W. 12th Street
New York, NY 10011
741-5690

Speech Communication Analysis, Inc.
222-0713

The following list consists of some of the most well known schools in the United States, along with other New York City institutions offering professional training. All the schools returned questionnaires stating that they would accept non-full-time students.

Code

INST   Institution

ADDR   Address and telephone number

CONT   Contact person, including telephone extension

COURS   Course offerings useful to professional singers

LANG   Language instruction offered

DICT   Languages in which diction instruction is offered

FEES   Amount required per semester for matriculation, registration, etc.

TUIT   Cost of instruction for credit or semester hour

SCHO   Availability of scholarship assistance

COMM   Additional comments

INST   CITY COLLEGE OF THE CITY UNIVERSITY OF NEW YORK
ADDR   Shepard 315A, 138th Street & Convent Avenue, New York, NY 10031   690-5411
CONT Professor Hanning; **COURS** Voice, vocal coaching, acting, stage movement, dance, fencing, keyboard, theory, history, musicianship, jazz, popular vocal; **LANG** English, French, German, Greek, Italian, Russian, Spanish; **DICT** English, French, German, Italian; **FEES** $50; **TUIT** $295; **SCHO** For full-time students only

INST   DALCROZE SCHOOL OF MUSIC
ADDR   161 E. 73rd Street, New York, NY 10021   879-0316
CONT Voice, solfege, theory, Dalcroze Method; **TUIT** $360 for students enrolled in classes; $450 for students taking private instruction only
COMM The only institution in America that grants Dalcroze certificates.

INST   HUNTER COLLEGE OF THE CITY UNIVERSITY OF NEW YORK
ADDR   695 Park Avenue, New York, NY 10021   570-5736

CONT Professor George Stauffer, Graduate Adviser, 570-5735; **COURS** Orchestra, stage band, jazz workshop, collegium musicum, chamber music workshop, chorus; **LANG** English, French, German, Greek, Hebrew, Italian, Latin, Polish, Portuguese, Russian, Spanish, Swahili, Ukrainian, Yoruba; **FEES** $26.50; **TUIT** For courses, $95 per credit hour; for music lessons with private instructors, their fees; **SCHO** For qualified students

COMM Diction study at The Mannes College of Music.

INST THE JUILLIARD SCHOOL
ADDR Lincoln Center, New York, NY 10023   799-5000
CONT Miss Anderson (Office of Admissions); **COURS** Voice, vocal coaching, opera workshop, oratorio, early music, acting, stage movement, dance, fencing, keyboard; **LANG** English, French, German, Italian; **DICT** English, French, German, Italian; **FEES** $100; **TUIT** $5,000; **SCHO** For full-time students only

INST MANHATTAN SCHOOL OF MUSIC
ADDR 120 Claremont Avenue, New York, NY 10027   749-2802
CONT Paul Wolfe, Director of Admissions, Ext. 445; **COURS** Voice, coaching, opera workshop, early music, stage movement, keyboard; **LANG** Italian; **DICT** English, French, German, Italian; **FEES** $115 per semester; **TUIT** $230 per credit hour; **SCHO** For full-time students only

COMM Part-time study is not encouraged.

INST THE MANNES COLLEGE OF MUSIC
ADDR 157 E. 74th Street, New York, NY 10021   737-0700
CONT Dr. Richard Cuckson, Dean; **COURS** Voice, sightsinging, coaching; **LANG** French, German, Italian; **DICT** French, German, Italian; **FEES** included; **TUIT** $5,000 per year; **SCHO** Some, through auditions

COMM Ensembles, master classes, audition techniques, early music, camerata

INST NEW YORK SCHOOL FOR COMMERCIAL MUSIC INC.
ADDR 196 Bleecker Street, New York, NY 10012   473-3476
CONT Stan Persky, Director; **FEES** $15; **TUIT** $145 per course

COMM Every course is directed toward preparing students for auditions and for doing a professional job.

INST NEW YORK UNIVERSITY—SCHOOL OF EDUCATION, HEALTH, NURSING AND ARTS PROFESSIONS

ADDR   25 W. 4th Street, New York, NY 10003   598-3491, 598-3492

CONT Dr. Lily McKinley, 598-3493; **COURS** Voice, opera workshop, performance practice, choral conducting; **FEES** $25 plus $11 per point; **TUIT** $193 per point; **SCHO** None for part-time students

Other language instruction at Washington Square School of Arts and Sciences, School of Continuing Education.

Elizabeth Arrigo
874-0998
Teaches sight-reading of commercial jingles.

Maurice Finnell Studios
25 E. 86th Street
New York, NY 10028
772-6215, 840-1234
Courses in sightsinging and basic musicianship.

Appendix B   Information

Center for Arts Information
625 Broadway
New York, NY 10012
677-7548

Established in 1976 as a comprehensive information service for the nonprofit
arts community in New York State. Primary objective is collection and dissem-
ination of information concerning services, programs and funds to aid in the
management, production and presentation of nonprofit arts. Maintains a research library of books, periodicals, organization files and subject files. Use
of the facilities is by appointment only.

The Foundation Center Library
888 Seventh Avenue
New York, NY 10009
975-1120

The center is a goldmine of information about money, grants and so forth.
(See more below under "Publications.")

Library and Museum of the Performing Arts at Lincoln Center
Lincoln Center
New York, NY 10023
870-1650 (Reference Desk)

Located to the right and slightly behind the main entrance of the Metropolitan
Opera House (between the Met and the Vivian Beaumont Theater). Recordings, tapes and listening facilities for records, as well as free concerts, lectures
and exhibits. A MUST!

The following publications are indispensable resources for the singer. For additional items, see the "List of Publications" printed by the Central Opera Service.

Newspapers

Backstage: The leading trade newspaper for performers in New York City. It contains listings and vital statistics for all major stage and musical productions in the city, as well as advertisements for instruction and services relevant to performers. Published weekly, on Thursdays, and sells for 75¢ at most city newsstands.

Billboard: Occasionally contains information of value to singers. Published weekly.

Show Business: Similar to *Backstage,* but sometimes less comprehensive in audition listings. Published weekly.

Variety: Infrequently contains listings and information useful to singers. Published weekly.

Magazines

Musical America: Published monthly in conjunction with *High Fidelity* magazine. The annual issue, published in January, contains fairly complete listings of opera companies, artists' managers, festivals, music schools, service and professional organizations, contests, foundations and awards, and other information essential to singers. Unfortunately, it costs $40 but is probably worth it. Can be purchased in most music stores and is available in libraries.

Opera News: Published by the Metropolitan Opera Guild, Inc., it contains listings of competitions, performances and many articles of interest to singers. Published 17 times per year. A year's subscription costs $30 and can be obtained by writing *Opera News,* Circulation Department, 1865 Broadway, New York, NY 10023.

Bulletins and Quarterlies

The three quarterlies listed below contain information valuable to singers, including current listings of U. S. opera company seasons.

Central Opera Service Bulletin
Metropolitan Opera, Lincoln Center
New York, NY 10023

Opera America Bulletin
633 E St., NW
Washington, DC 20004

Opera America also publishes a series of charts providing information about auditions for U.S. opera companies and various apprentice programs.

The Opera Quarterly
University of North Carolina Press
Box 2288
Chapel Hill, NC 27514

Annuals

Foundation Grants to Individuals: Published by The Foundation Center, 888 Seventh Avenue, New York, NY 10019, and edited by Claude Barilleaux and Alexis Teitz Gerzumky. It includes a few grants for performers that are not listed in *Career Guide for the Young American Singer.*

Money Business: Published by The Artist's Foundation, Inc., 110 Broad Street, Boston, MA 02110. This annual lists grants and awards for creative artists, but is primarily geared to the visual arts and pursuits other than singing.

Money for Artists: Published by the Center for Arts Information, 625 Broadway, New York, NY 10012. Although intended primarily for visual artists, it may include information helpful to performers. Price: $3. The Center for Arts Information publishes several additional brochures dealing with financial help for artists.

Musical America: International Directory of the Performing Arts
ABC Leisure Magazines, Inc.
The Publishing House
Great Barrington, MA 01230
Published annually. (See description under "Magazines.")

Places: A Directory of Public Places for Private Events and Private Places for Public Functions. Published by Tenth House Enterprises, Inc. Includes listings with contact information on auditoriums, recital and rehearsal spaces, mansions and other unique spaces that performers can rent. To order, send $16.95 plus $1.50 for first-class postage to Caller Box 810, Gracie Station, New York, NY 10028.

Summer Theater Guide: Compiled and edited by John Allen. This is a roundup of vital information about summer stock theaters that hire non-Equity performers. The most recent version cost $4.95 and was obtainable in theatrical bookshops.

Books: Recommended Aids

The Art of the Song Recital by Shirlee Emmons and Stanley Sonntag
Schirmer Books

Career Guide for the Young American Singer (COS Handbook)
Central Opera Service
Metropolitan Opera, Lincoln Center
New York, NY 10023
This guide, supplemented by a bimonthly addendum, is the most complete and up-to-date source of information on competitions, grants, awards and career opportunities. It is an absolute must for young singers.

The National Directory of Grants and Aid to Individuals in the Arts
Editors, Washington International Arts Letter
P.O. Box 9005
Washington, DC 20003

Towards a Career in Europe by Richard Owens
American Institute of Musical Studies
2701 Fondren Drive
Dallas, TX 75206
Contains information of interest to singers preparing to audition or study in Europe.

Word-by-Word Translations of Songs and Arias by Coffin, Scarecrow and Delattre
(Part I: German and French; Part II: Italian)
The Scarecrow Press, Inc.

Books: Saving Money in New York City

Bargain Finder: The Encyclopedic Money Saving Guide to New York City by Eric Zuesse, Golden-Lee Books

Five Hundred Things to Do in New York for Free by Brian Cox, New Century

Free New York by Anne and David Yeadon, Free City Books

The Hip Pocket Guide to New York by Tim Page, Harper and Row

New York Inflation-Fighter's Guide by Eileen Douglas, William Morrow and Company

New York on $25 a Day by Joan Hamburg and Norma Ketay, Frommer/ Pasmantier

New York Underground Gourmet by Milton Glaser and Jerome Snyder, Simon and Schuster

Where to: Find It, Buy It, Eat It in New York by Gerry Frank, Gerry's Frankly Speaking

Books: Personal Growth and Management

Getting Organized by Stephanie Winston, Warner Books

Getting Well Again by O. Carl Simonton and Stephanie Matthews Simonton, Bantam Books

What Color Is Your Parachute? by Richard Nelson Bolles, Ten Speed Press

Wishcraft: How to Get What You Really Want by Barbara Sher with Annie Gottlieb, Ballantine Books

Appendix C   Professional Resources

Binzer Music House
225 E. 85th Street
737-1146
11:00 A.M.–6:00 P.M., Mon.–Sat.

Colony Record & Radio Centre, Inc.
1619 Broadway
265-2050
9:30–2:30 (A.M.), Mon.–Fri.; 10:00–3:00 (A.M.), Sat.; 10:00–2:00 (A.M.),
Sun.

Frank Music Company
43 W. 61st Street, 24th floor
582-1999
10:00 A.M.–5:30 P.M., Mon.–Fri.; 12:00–5:00 P.M., Sat.

Lincoln Square Music Company, Inc.
2109 Broadway
742-7371, 724-7370

Metropolitan Opera Shop
Metropolitan Opera House
Lincoln Center
799-3100
10:00 A.M.–10:00 P.M., daily

Music Exchange
151 W. 46th Street, 10th floor
354-5858

Music Store at Carl Fischer
62 Cooper Square (7th Street & Third Avenue)
677-0821
10:00 A.M.–5:45 P.M., Mon.–Sat.

The Joseph Patelson Music House
160 W. 56th Street
582-5840
9:00 A.M.–6:00 P.M., Mon.–Sat.

Schirmer Music
40 W. 62nd Street
541-6236
10:00 A.M.–8:00 P.M., Mon.–Sat.

We strongly suggest that you request references from any piano tuner prior to admitting him to your apartment. The following list includes a few of the many tuners in the New York City area. In some cases they have submitted only their first names.

Len Greene
244-4270

Jim
595-1265

Peter R. Lewy
807-1094

Mark
591-0958

Larry Wolf
795-8599

Code

NAME   Name of hall

ADDR   Address and telephone number

CONT   Contact person

DESC   Description of hall with number of seats

FEES   Rental costs

OTHR   Other information

NAME   AMDA (American Musical & Dramatic Academy)
ADDR   Ansonia Hotel, 2109 Broadway   787-5300

NAME   ALICE TULLY HALL
ADDR   Lincoln Center, Broadway at 65th Street   580-8700
CONT Delmar Hendricks, Booking Manager; **DESC** 1,096 seats; **FEES** $1,200 plus labor charges

NAME   AVERY FISHER HALL
ADDR   Lincoln Center, Broadway & 65th Street   580-8700
CONT Delmar Hendricks, Booking Manager; **DESC** 2,738 seats; **FEES** From $725 to $3,000 per performance; $175 for three-hour rehearsal; plus labor charges

NAME   BARBIZON PLAZA THEATER
ADDR   106 Central Park South   247-7000
CONT Rental agent: Manhattan Life Insurance Company; **DESC** 160 seats

NAME   BROOKLYN ACADEMY OF MUSIC
ADDR   30 Lafayette Avenue, Brooklyn   636-4144
CONT John Miller, Theater Manager

NAME   CAMI HALL (formerly Judson Hall)
ADDR   165 W. 57th Street   397-6981
CONT Richard E. Hansen, Manager; **DESC** 240 seats; **FEES** Vary with time and day, from $120 to $225; **OTHR** Book at least one month in advance; $150 deposit.

NAME CARNEGIE HALL
ADDR 881 Seventh Avenue   903-9710
CONT Gilda Barlas Weissberger, Booking Manager; **DESC** 2,800 seats in main hall; 297 in recital hall

NAME ENSEMBLE STUDIO THEATRE
ADDR 549 W. 52nd Street   247-4982
DESC 99-seat theater with piano

NAME GENE FRANKEL THEATRE
ADDR 36 W. 62nd Street   581-2775
DESC 75 seats

NAME GRACE RAINEY RODGERS AUDITORIUM, METROPOLITAN
         MUSEUM OF ART
ADDR Fifth Avenue & 82nd Street   879-5500, ext. 3497
CONT Nancy Williams; **DESC** 750 seats; **OTHR** Museum's own concert series, called the Introduction Series, is run by Nancy Williams. She accepts resumes.

NAME GREENWICH HOUSE MUSIC SCHOOL
ADDR 46 Barrow Street, New York, NY 10014   242-4770
CONT John S. Winkleman, Director; **DESC** 80 seats in Renee Weiler Concert Hall; 30 in classroom; **FEES** $175 for concert hall and courtyard; varies for rehearsal space and classroom

NAME SOLOMON R. GUGGENHEIM MUSEUM
ADDR 1071 Fifth Avenue (between 89th and 90th streets)   860-1365
CONT Vaness Jalet; **DESC** 299 seats

NAME LIBRARY AND MUSEUM OF THE PERFORMING ARTS
         AT LINCOLN CENTER
ADDR 111 Amsterdam Avenue   870-1613, 930-0880
COMM Joan Canale; **DESC** 212 seats

NAME   M & P REHEARSAL STUDIO
ADDR   306 W. 38th Street   564-0001
DESC 99-seat theater

NAME   MERKIN CONCERT HALL, ABRAHAM GOODMAN HOUSE
                                                                362-8060
ADDR   129 W. 67th Street
DESC 457 seats; **FEES** $1,225; **OTHR** Includes everything except PR; 2½
hours of rehearsal

NAME   MUSEUM OF THE CITY OF NEW YORK
ADDR   Fifth Avenue at 103rd Street   534-1672
DESC 248 seats; **FEES** Vary; prime time, Sunday afternoon, costs $1,000

NAME   NEW LITTLE THEATER
ADDR   Basement of Greek Orthodox Church of the Annunciation,
           302 W. 91st Street   724-2304
DESC Small theater with piano and sound equipment; **FEES** $150 for one
performance; deposit of 50% of total; rehearsal costs $10 per hour

NAME   NEW-YORK HISTORICAL SOCIETY
ADDR   170 Central Park West   873-3400, ext. 42
CONT Karen Zukowski

NAME   QUEENS COLLEGE, RATHAUS RECITAL HALL
ADDR   65-30 Kissena Boulevard   520-7200
CONT Lawrence Ferrar, Campus Facilities Officer; **DESC** 220 seats

NAME   ST. CYRIL'S CHURCH HALL
ADDR   62 St. Mark's Place   674-3442

NAME   ST. PETER'S PERFORMING ARTS CENTER
ADDR   336 W. 20th Street at Eighth Avenue   691-4616
DESC 99 seats

NAME SYMPHONY SPACE, INC.
ADDR 2537 Broadway (at 95th Street)   864-1414
CONT Allan Miller, Artistic Director; Isaiah Sheffer, Artistic Director; or Linda Rogers, Managing Director; **DESC** 922 seatss; **FEES** Vary; none if performance is free

NAME THIRD STREET MUSIC SCHOOL SETTLEMENT
ADDR 233 E. 11th Street   777-3240
CONT Frederick Wise or MaryLou Francis; **DESC** 325 seats in auditorium; 70 in recital room

NAME TOMI INC.
ADDR 23 W. 73rd Street   787-3980
DESC Terrace Theater, 75–79 seats; Park Royal Theater, 99–130 seats; **OTHR** Steinway pianos available

NAME TOWN HALL
ADDR 123 W. 43rd Street   997-1003
CONT Larry Zucker; **DESC** 1,498 seats; **FEES** $2,742 on Sunday afternoons, including two-hour rehearsal and two-hour performance, lighting, tickets and staff. Concert liability insurance deposit is $1,000; stage labor, $350 extra; **OTHR** Box office service on day of concert, $75. Box office service one week before concert, $225. Piano rental (brand new Steinway), $150 including tuning. Recording and other equipment is extra.

NAME TRINITY SCHOOL
ADDR 139 W. 91st Street   873-1650

NAME TURTLE BAY MUSIC SCHOOL
ADDR 244 E. 52nd Street   753-8811
CONT Janet M. Robbins, Executive Director; **DESC** 175 seats; **FEES** Vary with function

NAME VILLAGE GATE THEATER
ADDR Bleecker and Thompson Streets   475-5120
DESC Two theaters; seating for 10–500; sound, lights and piano; rehearsals and auditions

NAME   VINEYARD THEATER
ADDR   309 E. 26th Street   683-0696
OTHR Available during July and August

NAME   WEST SIDE HALL
ADDR   2465 Broadway   877-9012

Abraham Goodman House
129 W. 67th Street (west of Broadway)
362-8060 (9:00 A.M.–4:30 P.M., Mon.–Fri.)
$5–$7 per hour for studios with piano; $10–$15 per hour for larger rooms

Rooms available during week, daytime and evenings. Closed from 4:30 P.M. on Friday till Monday.

Actors Equity Audition Center
165 W. 46th Street (2nd floor)
869-8548; 869-8530, ext. 302
$6.50 per hour; $26 per half-day; $52 per day

Manager Tony Nicosia and assistant Tom Yates run the busiest rehearsal/ audition space in the city. The spaces are rented only to Equity members and producers.

AMDA Studios (American Musical & Dramatic Academy)
Ansonia Hotel, 2109 Broadway
787-5300
5:00–11:00 P.M.
$10–$15 per hour
Contact: Steve Dornbusch

All studios contain new Kawai pianos; pay phone in lounge area.

American Theater of Actors
314 W. 54th Street
581-3044
$6 per hour

Three rooms; payment due at time of rental.

Amity Arts Center Studio
22 W. 15th Street (5th floor)
924-5295
9:30 A.M.–9:00 P.M., Mon.–Sat.; 11:00 A.M.–6:00 P.M., Sun.
Contact: Jerry Ames

Sidney Armus
54 W. 22nd Street (2nd floor)
243-2805
$7 per hour for larger studios; $5 per hour for smaller studios

Broadway Arts
1755 Broadway (at 56th Street)
587-7947
$6–$9 per hour
Contact: Fergus Hunter

Harlequin Rehearsal Studios
203 W. 46th Street (2nd floor)
582-0120
10:00 A.M.–11:00 P.M., Mon.–Fri.; 10:00 A.M.–8:00 P.M., weekends.
From $3.50 per hour

Pianos in every room, though not in great condition. Nice management.

Le Studio
152 W. 56th Street (2nd floor)
757-1941
$12 per hour
Contact: Edwige Val

All rooms have pianos. Payment due at beginning of rehearsal.

Letang School of Dance Rehearsal Studios
1595 Broadway (2nd floor)
974-9332
Open at 10:00 A.M.
$10 per hour, but varies
Contact: Henry Letang

All rooms have pianos.

Minskoff Rehearsal Studios
1515 Broadway at 45th Street (3rd floor)
575-0725
$12.50–$25 per hour, depending on size
Contact: Nan Cimater

Busy; very secure building.

Morelli Ballet Studios
69 W. 14th Street (3rd floor)
242-1903
10:00 A.M.–9:30 P.M., Mon.–Thurs.; 10:00 A.M.–8:00 P.M., Fri.; 10:00 A.M.–
4:00 P.M., Sat.
$7.50 per hour

Hard to find. Pay in full when making reservations.

Nola Sound Studios
250 W. 54th Street (11th floor)
582-1417
$7 per hour for small studio; $15 per hour for medium; $20 per hour for large
Contact: Al Wick

Seven studios with Steinways.

TOMI Inc.
23 W. 73rd Street (16th floor)
787-3980
Contact: Paul Lapinski

Two theaters, two piano/vocal rooms.

Showcase Studios
950 Eighth Avenue (at 56th Street)
586-7947
$6–$9 per hour
Contact: Fergus Hunter

Applause Theatre Books
100 W. 67th Street
496-7511
10:00 A.M.–7:00 P.M., Mon.–Sat.; 12:00–6:00 P.M., Sun.

Drama Bookshop, Inc.
723 Seventh Avenue (2nd floor)
944-0595
9:30 A.M.–6:00 P.M., Mon.–Fri.; 10:30 A.M.–5:00 P.M., Sat.

Theatre Arts Book Shop
405 W. 42nd Street
564-0402
10:00 A.M.–8:00 P.M., Mon.–Sat.; 12:00–5:00 P.M., Sun.

Theatrebooks, Inc.
1576 Broadway
757-2834
10:30 A.M.–6:00 P.M., Mon.–Fri.; 12:00–5:00 P.M., Sat.

Appendix D Business Services

The following photographers are familiar with theatrical photography, including publicity head shots. Most of them advertise regularly in *Backstage*. Make sure you get an accurate price list before having photos made or reproduced. Because of the complexities of pricing, we have not listed prices. We suggest you call several photographers before deciding which one to use.

Jim Beecher
260-3404

David Brown
734-0530
(No fee unless satisfied)

Bruce Cahn
807-1403

Richard Caliban
242-5598

Philip Calkins
924-2346

Michael Chan
460-8030

Cornell Photography
757-4825

Danny Darrow
873-5968

Steve de Muro
266-4771, 998-5323

Cora du Back
226-5197

Frank Giraldi
840-8225

Michael Goldstein
242-8234

Mark Graham
254-1653

Nick Granito
684-1056

Robert Haufrecht
937-7557

Bob Helsel
Stephanie Helsel
594-8813

David Hogan
369-4575

Lisa Kohler
799-7687

Janice McNeely
688-1360, 534-9039

Tom Monaster
935-0646

Karen Moody
288-4787

Newly Studio
947-1077

Joe O'Neill
749-7024

Art Paxton
966-0972

Hal Rifkin
431-4768

Steve Riley
278-3341

Kathy Swanson
734-9345

Julia Tapley
924-5684

Listed below are only two of the dozens of resume services available in New York City. Many others advertise regularly in *Backstage*.

Copy Right Copy Shop
25 W. 43rd Street, Lobby (between Fifth and Sixth avenues)
869-9665

Open until 11:00 P.M., Mon.–Fri.

Word processing, 100 copies, cut to 8 x 10.
$18 special with *Backstage* ad.

Flair Printing Corporation
8 W. 45th Street
575-0088

Professionally printed resumes—100 copies for $14.
Retyped in IBM Executive or Elite typefaces. Superb offset printing.
One-hour premium service available.
Mailing envelopes and boards—$9 per 100 or $6 per 50 sets.

All of the individuals listed below work regularly with income tax matters relating to persons in the arts.

Donald J. Aibel, Esq., P.C.
Tax Attorney
250 W. 57th Street, Suite 2001
New York, NY 10019
765-7532

Richard Philip Berman, Esq., Associates, P.C.
98-15 Horace Harding Expressway, Suite 17-G
Forest Hills, NY 11368
212/699-4878

Rubin L. Gorewitz & Co., P.C.
Certified Public Accountants
250 W. 57th Street, Suite 615
New York, NY 10107
581-5335

Lorraine Lerman
Tax Consultant
26 W. 39th Street
New York, NY 10018
719-3753

Richard A. Levine
Income Tax Service
161 E. 91st Street
New York, NY 10028
831-1332

Harry Linton and Marc Bernstein
250 W. 57th Street, Office 2403
New York, NY 10019
582-3133

Gordon Voorhees
(Enrolled to practice before the IRS)
420 Riverside Drive, Suite 3-B
New York, NY 10025
864-8006

Action Answering Service
134 W. 32nd Street
279-3870

Call Back Answering Service, Inc.
25 W. 45th Street
730-1188

Call Board New York Communications, Inc.
330 W. 42nd Street
244-3800

Omega Telephone Answering Service
679-1303

On Board Answering Service
35 W. 45th Street
382-3535

On Call Answering Service
250 W. 54th Street
541-9400

Standby Telephone Exchange Inc.
250 W. 54th Street, Room 811
541-7600

Star Answering Service
2067 Broadway, Room 27
799-9190

Starphone Answering Service
875 Avenue of the Americas, Suite 1001
279-1981

Talent Exchange Inc.
250 W. 54th Street, Room 800
586-6300

Appendix E　Performing

Cunard Line Ltd.
Bramson Entertainment Bureau Inc.
1440 Broadway
New York, NY 10018
354-9575

Takes a month. Accepts 8 x 10 photos and resumes. Goes through managers and agents. Accepts video tapes with recommendation. Uses different club acts. Applicants must have some club training and touring. No city showcases, Broadway or stock.

Norwegian American Lines
Danny Leone, Florida Office
P.O. Box 13110
Port Everglades Station
Ft. Lauderdale, FL 33316

Sun Line Cruises
Contact: Tina Smith
397-6400, ext. 408

Video tape preferable. Attention: Personnel Director. Resume and pictures accepted. Languages are important.

Home Lines Cruises, Inc.
Bramson Entertainment Bureau Inc.
1440 Broadway
New York, NY 10018
354-9575

Bahama Cruise Line
61 Broadway
New York, NY 10006

Send resume and picture to Attention: Personnel. If interested, they will contact you directly.

Code

NAME   Full name of group

ADDR   Mailing address and telephone number

COND   Conductor/musical director

CONT   Contact person for auditions and information

DESC   Description of group

RLOC   Rehearsal location if other than above

TOUR   Does organization tour?

PRYR   Number of performances per year

DUES   Membership fees

UNAF   Union affiliation

PAID   Are chorus members paid?

NAME   BROOKLYN PHILHARMONIA CHORUS
ADDR   30 Lafayette Avenue, Brooklyn, NY 11217   636-4120
COND Alexander Dashaw; **DESC** Concerts at Brooklyn Academy of Music and with the Brooklyn Philharmonic; **RLOC** St. Ann's Church in Brooklyn Heights; Tues., 7:10 – 10:00 P.M.

NAME   ENSEMBLE FOR EARLY MUSIC
ADDR   217 W. 71st Street, 10023   749-6600
COND Fred Renz

NAME   THE GREEK CHORAL SOCIETY
ADDR   1860 Broadway, 10023   757-5496
COND Dr. Dino Anagnost; **CONT** John Kordel, Business Manager; **DESC** Volunteer choral society which charges a fee for the season. Performs in New York, New Jersey and Connecticut; **RLOC** Milbank Chapel, Columbia University; **TOUR** A smaller group called the Metropolitan Singers, also volunteer, does some touring.

NAME   GREGG SMITH SINGERS
ADDR   c/o Walter Gould at Century Artist Bureau, 866 Third
Avenue, 10022   752-3920
COND Gregg Smith; **TOUR** Yes; **UNAF** AGMA

NAME   MASTERWORK CHORUS AND ORCHESTRA
ADDR   300 Mendham Road, Morristown, NJ 07960   201/538-1860
COND David Randolph

NAME   MUSICA SACRA
ADDR   150 W. 87th Street, 10024   874-3104
COND Richard Westenburg, Music Director; **CONT** Barbara Lapcek, Executive Director; **DESC** Professional chorus which performs regularly in Avery Fisher Hall and Cathedral of St. John the Divine; **PRYR** Minimum of 10 to 14; **UNAF** AGMA; **PAID** Yes

NAME   NEW AMSTERDAM SINGERS
ADDR   3222 Central Park West, 10025   663-0576
COND Clara Longstreth, Conductor; **DESC** Avocational chorus; **RLOC** Inner Church Street, 120th Street & Claremont Avenue; **PRYR** Six to ten; **DUES** $100 a year; some scholarships; **PAID** Soloists only

NAME   NEW YORK CHORAL SOCIETY
ADDR   165 W. 57th Street, 10019   972-0113
COND Robert DeCormier, Music Director; **CONT** Pamela M. Reich, President; **DESC** One of New York's largest groups; a volunteer organization. Performs in Carnegie Hall and elsewhere and uses many soloists; **TOURS** Mr. DeCormier has other, paid, professional touring groups.

NAME   92ND STREET Y CHORALE
ADDR   1395 Lexington Avenue, 10028   427-6000
COND Amy Kaiser; **CONT** To audition, call the office in early fall.

NAME   ORATORIO SOCIETY OF NEW YORK
ADDR   881 Seventh Avenue, Suite 504, 10019   247-4199
COND Lyndon Woodside, Music Director; **CONT** Joseph Brinkley, Chairman and President; **DESC** One of New York's oldest performing organizations. A

volunteer group which presents several concerts a year in Carnegie Hall. Sponsors an oratorio contest each spring (contact Nick Nicosia); **TOUR** Occasionally; **UNAF** AGMA (for soloist contracts)

NAME ORPHEON CHORALE
ADDR c/o Andel Management Associates, 1860 Broadway,
          Suite 1714, 10023   757-5496
COND Dr. Dino Anagnost, Music Director and Conductor; **CONT** John Kordel, Business Manager; **DESC** Professional chorus which performs regularly with the Little Orchestra Society in Alice Tully Hall and in Carnegie Hall; **TOUR** Occasionally; **UNAF** AGMA

NAME SINE NOMINE SINGERS
ADDR c/o Peggy Friedman   431-1088
COND Harry Saltzman; **DESC** Semi-professional group

NAME WAVERLY CONSORT
ADDR 305 Riverside Drive, 10025   666-1260

The following list contains most of the churches in Manhattan that perform music with guest soloists. Whenever possible, we have included the names of individuals to contact regarding the music program. Many of them work with agents, yet in many instances the agents are not consulted.

Baptist

Abyssinian Baptist Church
Dr. Thompson
132 W. 138th Street
862-7474

Calvary Baptist Church
Paul Liljestrand
123 W. 57th Street
975-0170

(or contact Mr. Liljestrand at 914/358-1710)

Convent Avenue Baptist Church
Howard R. Mann
420 W. 145th Street
234-6767

(or contact Mr. Mann at 63 Hamilton Terrace #27, New York, NY 10031, 926-7976)

Madison Avenue Baptist Church
30 E. 31st Street
685-1377

Episcopal

All Angels Church
Charles Ennis
251 W. 80th Street
362-9300

All Saints Church
Rev. Dennis G. Michno
230 E. 60th Street
758-0447

Calvary Episcopal Church
Calvion Hampton
61 Gramercy Park North
475-1216

Cathedral Church of St. John the Divine
Richard Westenburg
Amsterdam Avenue & 112th Street
678-6888

Church of the Ascension
Dennis Keene
Fifth Avenue at 10th Street
254-8620

(or contact Mr. Keene at 12 W. 11th Street, New York, NY 10011)

Church of the Epiphany
John Cartwright
1393 York Avenue
737-2720

Church of the Heavenly Rest
Charles Dodsley Walker
2 E. 90th Street
289-3400

Church of the Incarnation
Jon Dillock
209 Madison Avenue
689-6350

Church of the Resurrection
Steve Rumpf
152 E. 74th Street
879-4320

Church of St. Mary the Virgin
Quentin Lane
145 W. 46th Street
869-5830

Church of the Transfiguration
John Morris
1 E. 29th Street
684-6770

(boys and men only)

Grace Church
Frank C. Smith
802 Broadway
254-2000

St. Bartholomew's Church
James Litton
Park Avenue at 51st Street
751-1616
(or contact Mr. Litton at 109 E. 50th Street, New York, NY 10022)

St. Clement's Episcopal Church for the Theater
Michael Burke
423 W. 46th Street
246-7277

St. George's Episcopal Church
209 E. 16th Street
475-0830
(volunteer choir only)

St. James' Episcopal Church
Alec Wyton
865 Madison Avenue
288-4100

St. John's in the Village
Ed Miller
224 Waverly Place
243-6192

St. Mark's Church in the Bowery
10th Street & Second Avenue
674-6377
(volunteer choir only)

St. Michael's Episcopal Church
Robert Barrows
225 W. 99th Street
222-2700

St. Paul's Chapel of Trinity Church Parish
Larry King
Broadway & Fulton Street
285-0874
(or contact Mr. King at 74 Trinity Place, New York, NY 10006)

St. Stephen's Episcopal Church
Robert Russell
120 W. 69th Street
787-2755

Lutheran

Holy Trinity Lutheran Church
Frederick O. Grimes
Central Park West & 65th Street
877-6815

St. Luke's Lutheran Church
Walter Hilse
308 W. 46th Street
246-3540

St. Peter's Lutheran Church
Gordon Jones
619 Lexington Avenue
935-2200

Nondenominational

Riverside Church
Riverside Drive & 122nd Street
222-5900

Presbyterian

Brick Church
Dr. Charles T. Lee
62 E. 92nd Street
289-4400

Central Presbyterian Church
Charles Pilling
593 Park Avenue (at 64th Street)
838-0808

Church of the Master
Alston Lambert
86 Morningside Avenue
666-8200

Fifth Avenue Presbyterian Church
William Whitehead (Director)
Richard Bouchett (Organist)
7 W. 55th Street
247-0490

First Presbyterian Church of New York
Dr. Robert Baker
12 W. 12th Street
675-6150

Madison Avenue Presbyterian Church
John Weaver
Madison Avenue at 73rd Street
288-8920

Rutgers Presbyterian Church
Marshall Williamson
236 W. 73rd Street
877-8227

Second Presbyterian Church
Harold Stover
6 W. 96th Street
749-1700

West End Presbyterian Church
165 W. 105th Street
663-2900

West Park Presbyterian Church
Grady Wilson
165 W. 86th Street
362-4890

Reformed in America (Collegiate)

Bethany Church
Rick Parks
400 E. 67th Street
734-0828

Marble Collegiate Church
Alden Clark
Fifth Avenue & 29th Street
686-2770

Middle Collegiate Church of Collegiate Reformed Dutch Church
Suzannah Gordon
Second Avenue at 7th Street
477-0666

West End Collegiate Church
Allan Seaver
368 West End Avenue
787-1566

Roman Catholic

Church of Our Saviour
Will Carter
59 Park Avenue
679-8166
(Mr. Carter can be reached there on Sundays, or a message can be left for him)

St. Agnes' Rectory
Cathy Beck (Organist)
143 E. 43rd Street
682-5722

St. Francis of Assisi Monastery & Church
Father Florian
135 W. 31st Street
736-8500

St. Ignatius Loyola Church
Johannes Somary
980 Park Avenue
288-3588
(or leave a message with Mr. Somary's answering service at 884-5547)

St. Jean Baptiste Church
Father Camire
184 E. 76th Street
288-5082

St. Patrick's Cathedral
John Grady
321 E. 50th Street
753-2261

St. Paul the Apostle Church
Father Ilecki
415 W. 59th Street
265-3209

(or Father Ilecki can be reached at 580-7513)

St. Vincent De Paul Church
Daniel Pross
116 W. 24th Street
243-4727

(or Mr. Pross may be reached at 201/434-4294)

St. Vincent Ferrer Church
Jim Christiansen (Organist)
869 Lexington Avenue
744-2080

Unitarian–Universalist

Community Church of New York
Arthur Frantz
40 E. 35th Street
683-4988

Unitarian Church of All Souls
Walter Klaus
1157 Lexington Avenue (at 80th Street)
535-5530

Universalist Church of New York City
Richard Marshal
4 W. 76th Street
595-8410

United-Methodist

Christ Church United Methodist
Dr. Donald MacDonald
Park Avenue at 60th Street
838-3036

Park Avenue United Methodist Church
Lyndon Woodside
106 E. 86th Street
289-6997

St. Marks United Methodist Church
Dr. Jay W. Sanford
55 Edgecombe Avenue
926-4400

Synagogues and Temples

Central Synagogue
Jim Christiansen (Organist)
or Cantor Richard Botton
123 E. 55th Street
838-5122

Congregation Habonim
44 W. 66th Street
787-5347

Congregation Kehilath Jeshurun
Cantor Davis
125 E. 85th Street (at Park Avenue)
724-1000

Congregation Shearith Israel
 Leon Hyman
Central Park West at 70th Street
873-0300
(all men)

Hebrew Tabernacle Congregation
Frederick Herman
607 W. 161st Street
568-8304

Metropolitan Synagogue of New York
Cantor Norman Atkins
40 E. 35th Street
679-8580

Park Avenue Synagogue
David Lefkowitz
50 E. 87th Street
369-2600

Stephen Wise Free Synagogue
Ellen Stettner Math
30 W. 68th Street
877-4050

Temple Israel of the City of New York
Robert Abelson
112 E. 75th Street
249-5000

Temple Shaaray Tefila
Bruce Ruben
250 E. 79th Street
535-8008

Many of the church and synagogue jobs in New York City are handled by "church agents." The three agents listed below seem to be the most active ones. They will ask you to sight-read at auditions.

Ann Bynum
116 Pinehurst Avenue, 10033
923-6312

Cindy Hewes
c/o Musica Sacra
20 W. 86th Street, 10024
595-9026

Jacqueline Pierce
212 W. 80th Street, 10024
799-6624

Most of the opera-producing organizations in the New York metropolitan area are listed below. The information provided—including the comments—came directly from the organizations.

Code

NAME   Name of opera company

ADDR   Address and telephone number

CONT   Contact person

AUDT   Auditions

ALOC   Audition location

TYPE   Type of operas produced:
                VP   —Verdi-Puccini
                BC   —Bel Canto
                O   —Operetta
                G&S —Gilbert & Sullivan
                RW —Rare Works
                AW —American Works
                CW —Chamber Works

LANG   Language in which operas are sung

PRYR   Number of productions per year

TOUR   Does company tour?

VIDO   Does company use video equipment?

UNAF   Union affiliation

PAID   Are chorus members paid?

PFEE   Are soloists charged a fee to perform with company?

WKRH   Number of rehearsals per week

LENG   Length of rehearsals

BNFT   Type of coaching provided

COMM   Comments

NAME   AMATO OPERA THEATRE, INC.
ADDR   319 Bowery, New York, NY 10003   212/228-8200
CONT Anthony Amato; **AUDT** 4 times/yr; **ALOC** New York; **TYPE** VP, BC,G&S,

RW; **LANG** Mixture; **PRYR** 6, Sept. – June; **TOUR** Y; **VIDO** Y; **PFEE** N; **WKRH** Varies; **LENG** 4 hrs

NAME APOLLO OPERA & DRAMA COMPANY, INC.
ADDR 2130 Broadway, New York, NY 10023   212/874-0392
CONT Nococlis Moraitis, Director/Phyllis Tarter, Assistant Director; **AUDT** Periodically; **ALOC** New York; **TYPE** RW, Tosti concerts; **LANG** I, F; **PRYR** 1 concert & 4 plays; **TOUR** N; **VIDO** Y; **PAID** Y; **PFEE** N; **WKRH** As needed; **LENG** Varies; **BNFT** Vocal & language coaching

COMM We produced seven rare operas in original language & recently moved to classical drama, producing three Moliere comedies & one Racine tragedy translated into English.

NAME ASSOCIATION FOR THE FURTHERMENT OF BEL CANTO
ADDR 11 Riverside Drive, New York, NY 10023   212/877-1595
CONT Stefan Zucker; **TYPE** BC, RW; **LANG** I, F; **TOUR** Y; **UNAF** AFM; **PAID** Y; **PFEE** N

COMM Primary focus is on recording, consisting largely of Bellini & contemporaries. We also undertake outside recording projects & record distribution. We perform in a major New York hall each season.

NAME BROOKLYN OPERA SOCIETY
ADDR Borough Hall, Room 400-A, Brooklyn, NY 11201   212/643-7115
CONT Rinaldo Tazzini, General Manager; **AUDT** By announcement; **ALOC** New York; **TYPE** VP,BC,AW; **LANG** Mixture; **PRYR** 3; **TOUR** Y; **VIDO** Y; **PAID** Y; **PFEE** N; **WKRH** 3–4 weeks; **LENG** 4 hrs

COMM The newest major regional professional opera company in New York. It has produced 81 full-scale performances & 17 major productions; it produced the first opera for TV shot on location in U.S., *Mme. Butterfly*.

NAME BROQUE OPERA COMPANY
ADDR 216 East 82nd Street, #19, New York, NY 10028   212/535-6069
CONT Marie King, Director/Dominic Meiman, Music Director; **AUDT** Fall; **ALOC** Varies; **TYPE** RW, CW; **LANG** E; **PRYR** 1–5; **TOUR** Y; **VIDO** Y; **UNAF** None; **PAID** Y; **PFEE** N; **WKRH** Varies, 4–10; **LENG** Varies; **BNFT** All forms of coaching are available to company members.

COMM Those interested in auditioning should send picture & resume to the company. When there is a need for a specific role, we will call you to set up time. Please don't call us. Just send a picture & resume.

NAME   CHAUTAUQUA OPERA, C/O C. AUERBACH
ADDR   315 W. 70th Street, New York, NY 10023
(or Chautauqua, NY 14722)   716/357-6286
CONT Cynthia Auerbach, Artistic Director, Winter phone 212/942-0553; **AUDT**
Fall & winter; **ALOC** New York, Chautauqua; **TYPE** VP, BC, O, RW, AW, CW;
LANG E; **PRYR** 4; **TOUR** N; **VIDO** N; **UNAF** AGMA; **PAID** Y; **PFEE** N; **WKRH**
2–3 weeks; **LENG** 30 hrs/week; **BNFT** Coaching in acting, movement, interpretive music
COMM Offers two summer programs for young singers: AGMA apprentice
program, and non-AGMA studio workshop for singers 20–26, including workshops & opportunity to perform in chorus of productions & individual scenes.

NAME   FAMILY OPERA
ADDR   P.O. Box 7234, North Bergen, NJ 07047   201/869-5534
CONT Josephine Ruffino, President/Dr. Herman Schlisserman, Musical Di-
rector; **AUDT** Performance season; **ALOC** NJ or studio of applicant; **TYPE**
VP, BC, O, AW; **LANG** I, F, E; **PRYR** 8; **TOUR** N; **VIDO** Y; **UNAF** None; **PAID**
N; **PFEE** N; **WKRH** 1–5 weeks; **LENG** 2 hrs
COMM A professional voluntary organization which performs in a professional
theatre with full orchestra, chorus, ballet, costumes & scenery & issues a
printed program at each performance.

NAME   GLIMMERGLASS OPERA THEATRE
ADDR   P.O. Box 191, Cooperstown, NY 13326   607/547-2255
CONT Paul Kellogg, General Manager/Charles Schneider, Music Director;
AUDT October, December; **ALOC** New York; **TYPE** C, VP, BC, O, G&S; **LANG**
E; **PRYR** 3; **TOUR** N; **VIDO** N; **UNAF** None; **PAID** N; **PFEE** N; **WKRH** 2
weeks

NAME   ISRAEL NATIONAL OPERA
ADDR   Am. Rep.: Albert Kay Associates,
58 W. 58th Street, New York, NY 10019   212/593-1640
CONT Mr. Simcha Evan Zohar; **AUDT** Year-round; **ALOC** Israel, New York;
TYPE C, VP, BC, O, RW, AW, CW; **LANG** I, F, Hebrew; **PRYR** 50; **TOUR** Y;
VIDO Y; **UNAF** Israel; **PAID** N; **PFEE** N; **WKRH** 2–5 weeks; **LENG** Depends
COMM Company activities temporarily suspended.

NAME   LAKE GEORGE OPERA FESTIVAL
ADDR   P.O. Box 425, Glens Falls, NY 12801   518/793-3858

CONT Paulette Haupt-Nolen, General Director; **AUDT** As needed; **ALOC** New York & major U.S. cities; **TYPE** VP, BC, RW, AW, Musical Theater; **LANG** E; **PRYR** 4 in summer, 1 during year; **TOUR** Y; **VIDO** Y; **UNAF** AGMA; **PAID** Y; **PFEE** N; **WKRH** Full schedule; **LENG** AGMA agreed; **BNFT** Coaching in acting, dance/movement, and other

COMM Strong acting skills required. We sponsor American Lyric Theater, a rigorous three-year apprentice program emphasizing acting disciplines.

NAME LIGHT OPERA OF MANHATTAN
ADDR 334 E. 74th Street, New York, NY 10021   212/535-6310
CONT William Mount-Burke, Producer/Director; **AUDT** Frequently during year; **ALOC** New York

NAME METROPOLITAN OPERA COMPANY
ADDR Metropolitan Opera House, Lincoln Center, New York, NY 10023   212/799-3100
CONT Lawrence Stayer; **AUDT** Frequent; **ALOC** New York; **TYPE** VP, BC, RW; **TOUR** Y; **WKRH** 6

NAME NEW YORK CITY OPERA
ADDR New York State Theater, Lincoln Center, New York, NY 10023   212/870-5600
CONT Donald Hassard, Music Administrator; **AUDT** Periodically; **ALOC** New York; **TYPE** VP, BC, O, G&S, RW, AW, CW; **LANG** Mixture; **PRYR** 17–19; July–November; **TOUR** Y; **VIDO** N; **UNAF** AGMA & other; **PAID** Y; **PFEE** N; **WKRH** Repertory; **LENG** Varies

NAME NEW YORK CITY OPERA NATIONAL COMPANY, C/O NEW YORK CITY OPERA
ADDR New York State Theater, Lincoln Center, New York, NY 10023   212/870-5635
CONT Nancy Kelly, Administrative Director; **AUDT** As needed; **ALOC** New York; **TYPE** VP; **LANG** Original; **TOUR** Y; **UNAF** AGMA; **PAID** Y; **PFEE** N; **WKRH** 6; **LENG** 6 hrs; **BNFT** Musical coaching

NAME NEW YORK GILBERT & SULLIVAN PLAYERS
ADDR 251 W. 91st Street, #4-C, New York, NY 10024   212/873-8660
CONT Al Bergeret, Artistic Director/Charles Pye, Administrative Director;

AUDT Adver. in *Backstage;* **ALOC** New York; **TYPE** G&S; **LANG** E; **PRYR** 4; **TOUR** Y; **VIDO** Y; **UNAF** None; **PAID** Y; **PFEE** N; **WKRH** 3; **LENG** 3–4 hrs

NAME   NEW YORK LYRIC OPERA COMPANY
ADDR   124 W. 72nd Street, New York, NY 10023   212/874-0351
CONT Donald Johnston, General Director; **AUDT** September; **ALOC** New York City; **TYPE** C; **LANG** E; **PRYR** 2–3; **TOUR** N; **VIDO** Y; **UNAF** Equity; **PAID** Y; **PFEE** N; **WKRH** 7 + 3 wks; **LENG** 3–4 hrs; **BNFT** Musical coaching provided

NAME   NEW YORK OPERA REPERTORY THEATRE, INC.
ADDR   670 West End Avenue, Apt. 12-E, New York, NY 10025
                                                                  212/874-7177
CONT Leigh Gibbs Gore, General Director/Ross Barentyne, Artistic Administrator; **AUDT** As need arises; **ALOC** Upper West Side; **TYPE** AW, CW; **LANG** E; **PRYR** 2–3; **TOUR** Y; **VIDO** N; **UNAF** Y; **PFEE** N; **WKRH** 3–4; **LENG** 3 hrs
COMM No chorus has been used yet, but members would be paid. Company plans a tour in northeastern U. S. for 1983–84 season.

NAME   THE OPERA ENSEMBLE OF NEW YORK, AT THE
                 LILLIE BLAKE SCHOOL
ADDR   45 E. 81st Street, New York, NY 10028   212/288-1485
CONT John Sheehan, Production Director/Ruth Bierhoff, Artistic Director; **AUDT** Fall, winter, spring; **ALOC** New York; **TYPE** C, VP, BC, O, RW, AW, CW; **LANG** Mixture; **PRYR** 3; **TOUR** Y; **VIDO** Y; **UNAF** None; **PAID** Y; **PFEE** N; **WKRH** 3–5; **LENG** 3–6 hrs; **BNFT** Vocal and dramatic coaching provided
COMM This is a Singer's Company dedicated to helping young singers who have potential to better develop, both vocally & artistically.

NAME   OPERA IN A SUITCASE
ADDR   793 14th Avenue, Paterson, NJ 07504   201/742-2892
CONT Theresa Minnocci; **AUDT** Upon request; **ALOC** Paterson, NJ; **TYPE** C, VP, AW; **LANG** Mixture; **PRYR** 1 opera & several education programs; **TOUR** Y; **VIDO** N; **UNAF** None; **PAID** N; **PFEE** N; **WKRH** 2–3 weeks; **LENG** Varies; **BNFT** Coaching provided
COMM If a production is sold to another organization, such as a school, performers are paid a nominal fee.

NAME OPERA ORCHESTRA OF NEW YORK
ADDR 170 W. 74th Street, Suite 101, New York, NY 10023   212/799-1982
CONT John D. Broome, Business Manager/Eve Queler, Music Director; **AUDT** Varies; **ALOC** Varies—New York; **TYPE** VP, BC, RW; **LANG** E, I, F, G, mixture; **PRYR** 3; **TOUR** N; **VIDO** Y; **UNAF** AGMA; **PAID** Y; **PFEE** N; **WKRH** 1 week prior; **LENG** Varies; **BNFT** Coaching
COMM Do concert performances.

NAME OSWEGO OPERA THEATRE, INC.
ADDR 10 Draper Street, Oswego, NY 13126   315/343-8955
CONT James J. Soluri, Artistic Director; **AUDT** November; **ALOC** Oswego, Syracuse, NYC with Bronx Opera; **TYPE** C, VP, O, G&S, AW; **LANG** E; **PRYR** 1; **TOUR** N; **VIDO** N; **UNAF** None; **PAID** Y; **PFEE** N; **WKRH** 6 + 2 wks; **LENG** 3 hr; **BNFT** Coaching—vocal, acting & dance (as needed)
COMM Excellent technical resources & joint productions with Bronx Opera Company in alternate years. Recent productions: *Magic Flute, Susannah.* Professional orchestra. Stress use of young professional central New York performers.

NAME PINE ORCHARD ARTISTS FESTIVAL
ADDR Palenville, NY 12463   518/678-9286
CONT Jay Pouhe; **ALOC** New York; **TYPE** C, O, AW, CW; **LANG** E; **PRYR** 6; **TOUR** N; **VIDO** Y; **UNAF** None; **PAID** N; **PFEE** Y; **WKRH** 6–2 weeks; **LENG** Varies; **BNFT** Vocal coaching
COMM Company members should realize that this is a new company in a rural area, & that dedication to art form comes before monetary tribute.

NAME PITTSBURGH CHAMBER OPERA THEATRE
ADDR P.O. Box 71067, Pittsburgh, PA 15213   412/683-0725
CONT Mildred Miller Posvar, Artistic Director/Gretchen De Graff, Auditions Coordinator; **AUDT** Spring; **ALOC** Pittsburgh, New York; **TYPE** C, VP, CW, M; **LANG** E; **PRYR** 9 plus 4 shortened operas in schools; **TOUR** Y; **VIDO** N; **UNAF** None; **PAID** Y; **PFEE** Y; **WKRH** daily—2 wks; **BNFT** Vocal coaching

NAME REGINA OPERA COMPANY
ADDR 1251 Tabor Court, Brooklyn, NY 11219   212/232-3555
CONT Administrator, Marie Cantoni/Director, Alejandro Guzman, Fran Garber-Cohen; **AUDT** September, March, January; **ALOC** Regina Hall, 12th Avenue & 65th Street, Brooklyn; **TYPE** VP, BC, O; **LANG** Mixture; **PRYR** 3

operas & 5+ concerts; **TOUR** N; **VIDO** Y; **UNAF** None; **PAID** N; **PFEE** N; **WKRH** 2; **LENG** 3–9 wks; **BNFT** Vocal coaching

COMM Have done full productions for 12 years. Professional singers are used in leading roles & young professionals in comprimario roles. Most operas are done in original language. All roles are double cast.

NAME   ST. LUKE'S CHAMBER ENSEMBLE/CHILDREN'S
             FREE OPERA OF NEW YORK
ADDR   225 Lafayette Street, New York, NY 10012   212/226-1115
CONT Michael Feldman, Artistic Director/Marianne Lockwood, Executive Director; **AUDT** As needed; **ALOC** New York; **TYPE** C, RW, CW, M, O; **LANG** E; **PRYR** 3; **TOUR** N; **VIDO** N; **UNAF** None; **PAID** Y; **PFEE** N; **WKRH** 5–6; **LENG** 4–5 hr; **BNFT** Vocal coaching when necessary

COMM Performances are held in major halls: Brooklyn Academy of Music, Town Hall, Lehman Center—ten performances a week of a one-hour production with sets, costumes & full orchestra.

NAME   STATE REPERTORY OPERA
ADDR   363 W. South Orange Avenue, South Orange, NJ 07079
                                                                   201/763-7969
CONT Dita Delman, Artistic Director/James Sadewhite, Conductor; **AUDT** June & September; **ALOC** New York; **TYPE** BC, G&S; **LANG** Mixture; **PRYR** 2; **TOUR** Y; **VIDO** Y; **UNAF** None; **PAID** N; **PFEE** N; **WKRH** 2–12 wks; **LENG** 3 hr; **BNFT** Voice coaching, acting & dance

COMM We are a small company with an excellent reputation. We hire singers who are experienced & show potential. Acting ability is necessary.

NAME   TOMI INC.
ADDR   Park Royale Hotel, 23 W. 73rd Street, New York, NY 212/787-3980

NAME   THEATRE OPERA MUSIC INSTITUTE
ADDR   23 W. 73rd Street, New York, NY 10023   212/787-3980
CONT Thomas Lo Monaco & Lucy Greene, Artistic Directors; **AUDT** 2–3 mos. before performance; **ALOC** New York; **TYPE** VP, BC, RW, CW; **LANG** Mixture; **PRYR** 6–8; **TOUR** N; **VIDO** Y; **PAID** Y; **PFEE** Y; **WKRH** Varies, 4–8 wks; **LENG** As required; **BNFT** Occasional vocal, acting & dance coaching

NAME   TOURING CONCERT OPERA COMPANY, INC.
ADDR   228 E. 80th Street, New York, NY 10021   212/988-2542

CONT Director, Alberto Figols/Administrator, Priscilla Gordon de Figols; **AUDT** As needed; **ALOC** New York City; **TYPE** VP, BC, O, G&S, RW, AW, CW; **LANG** I & mixed; **PRYR** 8 or more; **TOUR** Y; **VIDO** Y; **UNAF** None; **PAID** Y; **PFEE** N; **WKRH** 3–4 wks; **LENG** 2–5 hrs; **BNFT** Coaching in acting, voice & dancing

COMM Hard working, good attitude on & off stage. Excellent musicians.

NAME   VIENNESE OPERETTA COMPANY OF NEW YORK, INC.
ADDR   400 W. 43rd Street, Suite 45-D, New York, NY 10036   212/695-1454

CONT Lois Albright, Honorary Board/Nicolai Gedda, Austrian Consulate, Advisory Board; **AUDT** Prior to production; **ALOC** New York; **TYPE** Strictly Viennese operetta; **LANG** E, G; **PRYR** 3–4; **TOUR** Y; **VIDO** N; **UNAF** Musicians; **PAID** Y; **PFEE** N; **LENG** 2–3 hrs

COMM Performers must be experienced.

Listed below are a few places in New York City where you can have the opportunity to sing and work. Some of them are "just to sing"—that is, customers can perform.

Asti Restaurant Inc.
13 E. 12th Street (off Fifth Avenue)
741-9105
Just to sing—mostly opera, some musical comedy.

Beefsteak Charlie's
1500 Broadway
398-1910
Singer-waiters/waitresses.
Broadway at 51st Street
757-3110
Singer-waiters/waitresses.

Bianchi & Margherita Restaurant
186 W. 4th Street (between Sixth & Seventh avenues)
741-9712
Just to sing—mostly opera, some Broadway music.

Il Cantone
294 Columbus Avenue
496-9226
Just to sing.

Mamma Leone's Ristorante
239 W. 48th Street (off Broadway)
586-5151
Just to sing.

Mrs. J's Sacred Cow Steak House
228 W. 72nd Street
874-8174
Singer-waiters/waitresses.

Something Different
1488 First Avenue
570-6666
Singer-waiters/waitresses.

By far the best way to get information on the various summer employment opportunities is to start watching *Backstage* in March, when job openings from Alabama to Alaska start to appear. We could not begin to list all the companies. Equity members can obtain notices of auditions for summer theaters directly from the union office. Additionally, the following organization may be helpful:

Strawhat Auditions
642 Amsterdam Avenue, #110
New York, NY 10025
222-1722

This organization auditions for an estimated 400 job openings on the "Straw-hat Circuit." *It is intended primarily for non-Equity performers, and most of the casting is for apprentices, interns and Equity membership candidates.* Write (do not call) for information.

Astroworld
Show Operations
9001 Kirby Drive
Houston, TX 77054

Busch Gardens/The Old Country
Entertainment Department
P.O. Drawer F-C
Williamsburg, VA 23185

Busch Gardens/The Dark Continent
Entertainment Department
3000 Busch Boulevard
Tampa, FL 33612

Walt Disney World
Talent Booking Office
P.O. Box 40
Lake Buena Vista, FL 32830

Disneyland
Entertainment Division
1313 Harbor Boulevard
Anaheim, CA 92893
(714) 999-4000

Hersheypark
Allan Albert
Hersheypark Entertainment
Hershey, PA 17033

Magic Valley Village
John Henson, Entertainment Manager
Magic Valley Park
Bushkill, PA 18324

Opryland
Entertainment Department
2802 Opryland Drive
Nashville, TN 37214

Six Flags Great Adventure
Show Operations
P.O. Box 120
Jackson, NJ 08527
(201) 928-2000, ext. 2201

Six Flags Magic Mountain
Show Operations
P.O. Box 5500
Valencia, CA 91355

Six Flags over Georgia
Show Operations
P.O. Box 43187
Atlanta, GA 30378

Six Flags over Mid-America
Show Operations
Box 666
Eureka, MO 63025

Six Flags over Texas
Show Operations
P.O. Box 191
Arlington, TX 76004

Taft Attractions
Entertainment Department
1932 Highland Avenue
Cincinnati, OH 45219
(513) 241-8989

Appendix F   Forms

Audition for:

at _____ , on _____
　　　(place)　　　　　　　(date)

Agency or theater: _____

Address and telephone number: _____

_____

Heard by _____ , _____ , _____

Clothing worn: _____

Repertoire offered/sung: _____

_____

_____

Repertoire requested: _____

_____

_____

General comments were: _____

_____

_____

Personal reactions to

singing: _____

the audition: _____

the place: _____

Further contact should be made on _____

Follow-up Record
(date)　　　　　　　(results)

Business Expenses

Union dues	$_____	Accounting fee for tax preparation $_____	
Union assessment	$_____	Photos	$_____
Costumes & uniforms	$_____	Publicity & advertising	$_____
Maintenance & cleaning of costumes & uniforms	$_____	Commissions to agents	$_____
		Instrument insurance	$_____
Maintenance & repairs of instruments	$_____	Printing, stationery, postage, mailers, office supplies & resumes	$_____
Makeup for performances	$_____		
Special hair-do's & beauty parlor expenses for performances	$_____	Business entertainment	$_____
		Business gifts	$_____
Phone service	$_____	Studio maintenance or rental	$_____
Phone used for business	$_____	Apt. rent for year	$_____
Telephone booth calls	$_____	_____% used for business	
Cabs & travel fares, one job to another in same day	$_____	Electricity for year _____% used for business	$_____
Records & tapes & scripts for profession	$_____	Business checks & charges	$_____
		Investment services	$_____
Music & books	$_____	Safe deposit box	_____
Substitutes for illness or conflicting engagements	$_____	Auto used for business only, one job to another on same day @ 20¢ per mile _____ miles	$_____
Trade papers & magazines	$_____		
Business tips to dressers, stagehands, etc.	$_____	Tolls	$_____
		Parking	$_____
Special coaching for particular performances to maintain & improve skills	$_____	Miscellaneous	$_____
Tickets for concerts & plays for profession	$_____		

DEPRECIATION

Item	Cost	Date Acq'd.	Prior Deprec.	Salvage Value	Method of Deprec.	No. of Years	Deprec. This Year	
								$_____

TOTAL BUSINESS EXPENSES $_____

Travel & Entertainment Expenses

1. Tour Expenses (not reimbursed) _____ days

    Lodging $ _____

    Food _____ per day including tips $ _____

    Laundry & cleaning $ _____

    Tips to porters, maids, etc. $ _____

    Local travel $ _____

    Telephone & miscellaneous $ _____

2. Tour Expenses (not reimbursed) _____ days

    Lodging $ _____

    Food _____ per day including tips $ _____

    Laundry & cleaning $ _____

    Tips to porters, maids, etc. $ _____

    Local travel $ _____

    Telephone & miscellaneous $ _____

3. Tour Expenses (not reimbursed) _____ days

    Lodging $ _____

    Food _____ per day including tips $ _____

    Laundry & cleaning $ _____

    Tips to porters, maids, etc. $ _____

    Local travel $ _____

    Telephone & miscellaneous $ _____

                                       Total $ _____

We at AIMS want this book to continue to be useful. We know that times change and that all our information must be updated occasionally. Completion of this form will be a great help to us and to singers who follow you. Please fill in the form, add more pages if you wish, and return to:

American Institute of Musical Studies
2701 Fondren Drive
Dallas, TX 75206

I found this book to be:
☐ a godsend   ☐ very helpful   ☐ fairly helpful   ☐ no help

I needed more information on:

_____

_____

_____

_____

_____

_____

_____

_____

_____

The following information (telephone numbers, etc.) I found to be incorrect:

_____

_____

_____

_____

_____

I purchased the book: ☐ prior to coming to New York.
                      ☐ soon after arrival in New York.
                      ☐ after a year or more in New York.
I have lived in New York for _____ years.
I would like to write for the book a chapter on _____

_____

Other suggestions: _____

_____

_____

_____

_____

_____

_____

_____

_____

_____

(Optional)
Name _____

Address _____

_____

Telephone _____